J S MAY

This is The Place

SLOW WAVE
PUBLISHING

First published by Slow Wave Publishing 2022

Copyright © 2022 by J S May

This is a work of non-fiction. Names, some places and other identifiers have been changed to provide anonymity.

First edition

ISBN: 978-1-7396859-0-4

*This book was professionally typeset on Reedsy.
Find out more at reedsy.com*

For my mother

Contents

Foreword

I started writing this book in 2005, a few weeks after I returned home from hitchhiking in Norway, although at that time I didn't know it was going to be a book—I just wanted to make a record of my time hitchhiking. I enjoyed writing about the things I'd seen and the people I'd met. I enjoyed it so much that when I was done, I went through my old travel journals and wrote the second story you have in this book, *Dexterity.* By the time I was planning my third travel anecdote, I realised that these stories were all part of a larger narrative that spanned nine years of my life. I decided to make them into a book.

Unfortunately, by this point the stories were written in such a way that it would have made no sense to rearrange them into chronological order, so I chose to line them up in the same order in which they were written, with a few alterations to make things a little clearer. Each story in some way influenced the one I wrote next, so I would argue that the chapters are ordered, if only in an unusual way. I found that writing about my walk to Spain was exhausting, so I broke it up. It appears in more or less the same broken-up order that I wrote it in.

I think that the book's present layout is the best one for it, even if it does get a little confusing at times. I think it fits; if you peeled open my head and stared inside my brain, into my spirit, you would not see a linear story. You would see a smashed-up mosaic of all the narratives that make me who I am; many tiny stories making up one larger one. I think this would be true of everyone, and it's also true of the places I've written about. Maybe even more so.

It's a funny thing cannibalizing your own life story and sense of self to make a book. I hope you like the end result. I've changed every name and omitted a few unimportant events, and my memory has probably changed other details without my consent. But I've done my best to be as honest as I can; because, I hope, you can do a lot with honesty.

—J M, November 2021

1

Imre and I

The Norway Hitch

The first time I saw Imre was when I was hitchhiking my way out of Trondheim. I was trying to get to a town called Steinkjer before 10 p.m. because that's when traffic usually dried up. He was standing in a bush on the side of the road wearing a long transparent anorak, which had angular shoulders and thinned in the middle like a woman's trench coat. He was tall and skinny, with ripped jeans that were faded and almost brown with dirt, and was leaning forward into the road holding a cardboard sign out in front of him. The sign was white and had "Mo i Rana" written on it in black marker, and in the middle of the O there was a smiley face. He was smiling serenely at the passing cars in a way that made me think he had mental health problems. I wondered how easy it was to get picked up looking like that.

I turned to my ride and said, "That's a bad spot. No one can stop to pick him up from there," and he agreed. My ride was called Anders. He was middle-aged and bald, with a bit of a gut, and so sensitive and kind that I could have cried when he talked about where he shopped to save money and the things he liked to do when he wasn't working. Like a lot of the Norwegian men I had met, Anders supported Leeds United and had a tattoo of the team's logo on his forearm.

Together we travelled forty kilometres north, until it was time for Anders to head east, and I got dropped off at a bus station in a town called Stjørdal. I moved my bag onto the curb, out of the way, to make sure that drivers could see the bus stop where they could pull in if they wanted to stop for me. I put my thumb out. I was opposite a Kiwi supermarket, and I thought about going over the road to check out the prices because it was one of the shops where I could get a cheap meal, but I didn't like the idea of leaving my spot and potentially missing a ride. It was only the early afternoon, but I'd been waiting a long time between rides in that part of Norway. I knew that if I was going to make the next one hundred kilometres to Steinkjer that day, I had to keep going.

I had only been there ten minutes when I saw him again, approaching from the other end of the road. He had taken his see-through women's raincoat off and tucked it over his satchel, and he had his cardboard sign under his arm. Someone must have picked him up from the hedge he had been standing in outside Trondheim and dropped him off fifty metres from where Anders had left me.

He strolled over to me, taking big loping steps, with his boots dragging along the ground because they weren't laced up properly. I could smell him before he was ten metres from me. He smelt like a bin. When he reached me, he started speaking in English, which was clear despite a heavy accent and a lisp.

"Hello, I'm Imre from Hungary, I'm hitching to Nordkapp," he said, and we shook hands formally.

He asked me where I was headed, and I told him I was trying to get to Alta, but that I hoped to make it to Steinkjer that night.

"I thought I'd try and get to Mo i Rana tonight," he said.

"Right."

"Is Alta in the north?"

"The very north."

"Not the very north," he said. "Nordkapp is the very north. If we're going the same way, maybe we should try joining forces and hitch together?"

"I don't know if people would stop for two men."

"We could try it for fifteen minutes and if we don't have any luck then I can go down and use the bus stop further on."

He put his sign out and leant into the road and started smiling vacantly again. I started smiling too. As the cars passed, I tried to make the people inside them laugh at the way I was smiling at them, and I thought about how part of what I like about hitchhiking is that people find it ridiculous.

"You have a big rucksack. Do you have a tent?" he asked me.

"Yes," I said, "don't you?" The only things he carried other than his tiny laptop satchel were his sleeping bag and the see-through women's raincoat.

"No, I used to have a tent, but I hated carrying it. I have my sleeping bag. I'd rather travel really light and just sleep in some bush."

"What about when it rains?"

"I use bus shelters, and some plants are pretty good. So far I've only had one really bad night and I just stayed awake for most of it."

Imre stood almost in the road with his sign out as he hitched. Some of the passing cars only just missed him. I could tell he wanted to talk but I didn't say anything to him. I kept my focus

3

on the road to avoid looking at him. After less than fifteen minutes, he said, "OK, I'll try that bus stop further on," and loped away. I felt guilty because it was probably my coldness that had made him leave. Not long after he'd left, a man in a Tesla stopped and took me fifty kilometres further north.

A few hours later, I was hitching from the entrance of a car park when a van passed me and turned around specifically to pick me up. The driver honked his horn from the other end of the car park, and I ran over to him with my rucksack only half on.

"I saw you as I passed but I was going too fast to stop," he said as he got out of the car and started moving stuff off the passenger seats. "I've done this before, here in Norway. Me and a friend tried it to get home this way and no one fucking stopped," he said, and then clicked his fingers, clapped his hands, and stuck both his middle fingers up at the remembered cars that had passed him without picking him up.

"So you know what it's like," I said, and he nodded as he opened the side of the van so that I could put my bag in. As I put my rucksack down, I looked back down the road at the oncoming cars and saw Imre running up towards us, laptop case hitched high on his shoulder. I couldn't work out where he'd come from.

"Is this your friend?" the driver asked as we watched him approach.

"Kind of. Do you mind if he comes as well?"

"No, no, it's fine. We have another seat." He seemed excited to help another person out.

"That's very kind. He's a nice guy but he smells a bit," I said.

"That's OK."

When Imre reached us, he went straight to the van driver, put

4

out his hand and said, "Hello, I'm Imre from Hungary and I'm hitchhiking to Nordkapp," and the driver shook it and said his name was Caesar.

"Your accent. You're Romanian?" asked Imre.

Caesar nodded and then told him to put his bags in the back. Then we all climbed into the cab and Caesar started driving us to Steinkjer along the E6; which, despite being the biggest road in that part of the country, had only two lanes: one heading north and one heading south. On either side of the road was a blend of farmland and woodlands, composed of tall evergreens and patches of shorter, rounder trees that lined the outskirts of the fields. Periodically, the road ran parallel to the fjordside, and the woodlands would falter and then vanish, and I could see right across the water, which was baby blue and bordered by rolling, low mountains.

Caesar had been living in Berlin for the past ten years but had left to find a better job in Norway. His wife didn't want to move with him, so he divorced her and left the next day. I told Caesar that I was sorry to hear that, but he didn't seem sorry about it himself. He gave us tips on how to use Facebook to find girls in any town we were travelling to. It turned out that Imre's father was born in a town in Romania that Caesar said he knew well. Apparently, there are a lot of Hungarians in Romania.

"Have you ever been to Romania?" Caesar asked us. We both told him we hadn't.

"Go. It's not true what you hear in the media, that there are so many gypsies. OK, there are some gypsies, but most the people are light-skinned, like me," and he lifted his arm and pinched his skin to show us his complexion. "And you have to see the mountains there. You think you've seen mountains here?" he asked rhetorically and pointed at the majestic snow-capped mountain range that surrounded us. "These are not mountains, they are joke. No, not joke. What is the word...laughable!" he said, raising his voice in the excitement of finding the right word, then clicking his fingers and clapping his hands again for emphasis. "To see real mountains in Europe you have to go to Romania. The food is also great. And the girls! You can't imagine. If you went as an English guy, you can't imagine, man."

Caesar dropped us off once we reached the outskirts of Steinkjer. When we got out, he went into the back of the van and took out a tin of nuts and some fruit and handed them to me. He was a really nice guy. I looked at the city and saw a few skyscrapers, and I said, "Oh, it's a pretty big town."

Caesar laughed. "This?" he said. "This one is a big town? You think it's a big town because everything is so spread out. That's how they do it here in Norway. They put one house here, then in another ten kilometres they put another one, and then fifteen kilometres down the road a few more and a supermarket, and they say" — and he clicked his fingers and clapped his hands — "here we have a town."

Imre and I walked through Steinkjer, which was made up of low, grey buildings spread thin amongst pine trees and grassy communal areas. It looked more Soviet than Scandinavian. When we got to the other side of the town centre, we put our thumbs out again and were picked up by a middle-aged guy called Thomas, who gave us a ride back out into the empty country. Then three teenage gangster types took us a few more kilometres north before leaving us at a bus stop in the middle of nowhere.

At the start of every journey, Imre introduced himself as "Imre from Hungary" and explained that he was hitchhiking to Nordkapp. Each time, once he had finished, he would look at me and I would introduce myself; and when I had finished, Imre would tell everyone that we had just met and had only just started travelling together, and I was glad of that. As we waited between rides, Imre and I talked and ate the food Caesar had given us. Traffic was almost non-existent, with one car passing us every twenty minutes.

Imre had left Hungary six months earlier and had hitched to a farm in Germany run by hippies. He stayed there a while, working for food and accommodation, and then he moved on to work in a similar place in France. He had left Hungary with no money whatsoever, but one of his rides had given him a twenty-krone coin, which he still had in his pocket. Imre told me that he planned on keeping it until he got home; that way, he could say he returned home richer than when he had left.

"This trip is different," he said. "The other times I've hitched I had somewhere I needed to reach. Like I was trying to get to one of the farms I volunteered on, or when I had to get to Denmark because I had a job waiting for me there. Those times I was just travelling, but this time it feels more like a journey."

"I love that feeling," I said. "I've had a lot of stuff going on recently. My dad's got cancer, and me and my girlfriend have been having a lot of problems. This morning, I decided I was going to see how far north I could get, and the guy who was on reception at the hostel told me that I should head to Alta; and when I walked out to get my first ride, I felt good for the first time in months, just because I'd decided on some arbitrary goal that was miles away."

"Maybe there's something about this trip that's healing," Imre said. "It's the North Cape." And then he looked up to the sky and shouted, "It's the end of the world!" with both his arms outstretched.

"I think I'll go all the way now," I said. "I'll try and get to Nordkapp too. I like the thought of getting as far north as possible."

"Did you work out how much further north Nordkapp is from Alta?"

"The map on my phone won't show the exact distance without the Internet, but I think it's probably two hundred kilometres."

"You should definitely do it, then. Where did you start hitching from?"

"Amsterdam."

"You will have come from Amsterdam to get to Alta, and that's like, what, three thousand kilometres? What's another two hundred after that?"

The traffic grew thinner, and we got so bored that we started pacing up and down our little patch of road. We agreed that if the traffic stayed light, it was going to take days to get to Nordkapp.

Eventually, a silver people carrier pulled up with two young men in it. One of them leant out the window and shouted over to us, "I'm sorry we can't take you because we don't have enough room. We have our beds in the back so there is nowhere for you to sit. But the last guy that we passed and couldn't pick up, he ended up getting picked up by a Porsche!"

"Where are you from?" Imre asked them.

"Austria," they said, and smiled and waved as they drove off.

We went back to pacing and talking. When I started hitching in Amsterdam, I had never planned to go further north than Trondheim; whereas Imre had always wanted to go to the northernmost point. I told him I still wasn't really sure what

Nordkapp was. I'd never heard of it until we met.

"It's just the most northern point of Europe. A peninsula," he said.

"Is it a town?"

"There might be one nearby, but I don't know if it's technically a part of Nordkapp. The bit everybody goes to is like a cliff that looks out over the sea. That's the bit that is the most northern point exactly. It's Norway, man. You don't travel around Norway if you want towns."

Imre told me about what he thought both Nordkapp and the road ahead would look like. He'd heard that Nordkapp itself was treeless and barren, as no trees could survive that far into the Arctic. He also said that he thought we'd pass into the Arctic Circle probably the following day, or the day after that, as the border sat roughly halfway between Trondheim and Nordkapp.

"So, from the Arctic Circle onwards we will have sunlight through all of the night as well as the day," he said, and I nodded in agreement, pretending that I already knew all about it.

We also talked about our private lives. Imre was going to read Scandinavian studies at university in Hungary the coming September, provided the grade boundaries were low enough, but he wouldn't know what the grade boundaries were for another couple of days. He had an obsession with learning new languages that I envied, and he talked in depth about the differences between Danish and Norwegian, as he could speak some Danish. His English was better than the average Brit's; and he told me that a few years earlier his brother, who was working as a programmer, had paid Imre to do some translating for a game he had worked on. When I told Imre that I was going to be studying nursing, I could tell he was amused.

"That's a very British thing, I think," he said. "You don't get male nurses in Hungary. In fact, the word nurse also means sister."

So I said, "Well, we have pretty good levels of sexual equality in the UK. Maybe it will take a few more years for you guys to catch up," and there was a satisfying silence while he looked annoyed, and we both paced without looking or talking to each other.

We were still pacing silently when the same silver people carrier from earlier pulled up next to us. One of the Austrians leant out the window and said, "We didn't want to leave you here. We're going to move our stuff in the back and make you some space." He got out and started shifting stuff around in the back, and then invited me to climb in and sit on the mattress with him while Imre climbed in the front next to the driver.

He was called Jay, like me, and his friend was called Paul. Jay spoke in soft, broken English. He told me that he and Paul had rented their car in Oslo and were heading to Nordkapp too. As we travelled, Jay chain-smoked Marlboro Whites, ashing out of a tiny crack in the window after each toke. I liked him immediately, and soon we were talking about personal stuff. He told me that he had caught his girlfriend in bed with another man, and I told him that I thought I had a bit of an idea of what that felt like.

"It fucking sucks," I said, and he nodded and looked like he wanted to cry but was too tired.

"Yeah, it really fucking sucks."

In the front of the van, Paul was talking to Imre, and I wondered if they had noticed his smell yet. Jay told me they were hesitant about picking people up because at the start of the trip someone had stolen Paul's camera. I said it was good that despite being robbed they were still trusting enough to pick people up.

"We got a few miles up the road and thought, 'What if it was us two who were left on the side of the road like you two were.' So we turned around," said Jay, and I said that I liked their way of looking at things. Paul asked us what we were talking about.

"I said that it's good that you're trusting enough to let two strangers in your car like this," I said.

"I am a superman," Paul said from the front of the car in a thick Austrian accent and completely without irony. "I have been asking God to send me a thief for this entire journey," and then he lifted his arms and pulled his sleeves to his shoulders so that I could see his bulging muscles, and said, "because I will make sure it is the death of the thief."

I looked at Jay and was glad to see that he watched all this with amusement and affection, and I felt less uncomfortable.

Jay taught me bits of German and I helped him with his English, and then after an hour of driving, we stopped so that Paul could wash in a stream, stripping down to his boxers in front of us. His body was as defined and as muscular as a bodybuilder's. Once Paul was finished, he and Jay spent some time talking to each other quietly in German, and I knew it was about the way Imre smelt. They seemed to reach an agreement and Jay came to talk to us.

"We can take both of you for another one hundred kilometres," he said, "but after that, we will go back to our old routine of one sleeping while the other one drives. So we will have only one space in the front of the car, so you will have to choose which one of you wants to do that. And that person can come with us all the way to Nordkapp. Maybe it would be better for you to come, Jay, because you're on a time limit, not like Imre." Then he pointed at Imre's filthy jeans. "Dirty trip?" Jay asked, and Imre laughed it off, completely unaware that they didn't want him in their car. We thanked them for the kind offer of a further lift and told them we'd think about it.

For the next leg of the drive, Paul and Jay switched seats, and Paul sat in the back with me while Jay drove. Paul had curly blonde hair that flopped over his eyes and a pretty, Aryan face that didn't seem to go with his body. He had what seemed to be quite a senior job with a big finance company in Vienna, and throughout the conversation he casually told me about the supermodels he was sleeping with. Paul told me that he and Jay were old friends from school, and that he had organised their trip spur-of-the-moment to cheer Jay up because he was worried about him after his breakup.

Despite his strangeness and the way he looked, Paul seemed very kind and he listened to what I had to say with intensity, and I liked that. We talked about Norway.

"Both me and Jay have said that we would like to live here," Paul said. "It's a really great country, and in Austria now we are having second-world problems. You can't say third-world problems, but in some parts of the city, if you leave your bag out on the floor next to you, you can be sure that the next immigrant that walks past will take it. The country is getting in such a bad way that the police are completely unable to stop a lot of crimes. They didn't grow up with these issues. There was no immigration then." There was an awkward silence that lingered for a minute before he shouted something to Jay in German. "I was just telling him to drive a bit slower," Paul said. "I said that there is no point in risking all of our safety for the sake of us getting there a few hours earlier."

As we talked, everything seemed to end up in some way related to immigrants. Paul spoke a lot about immigration into

France and said that the police had lost control over parts of Paris entirely.

"You don't hear about it on the news," he said, "but I am part of an organisation that is dedicated to spreading the truth," and he stretched out his black T-shirt so I could see what was on the front. It had a white phalanx helmet on it with "European Phalanx, preserving the European spirit" written along the bottom. "We are a network of patriots that ranges from Spain to Poland," he said. "We have our own newsletters dedicated to spreading the truth."

Paul and I spent the next one hundred kilometres together talking a lot about economics, and also about shitty bosses that we'd had and how much we liked Norway. Every now and again immigration would come up and I would start talking about something else. Periodically, Paul would shout something to Jay in German and Jay would slow down, even though he wasn't really driving that fast. Paul told me that although he could be a fast driver, he would often drive well below the speed limit if he was in a residential area where there were women or children around. Towards the end of the journey, we talked about the possibility of killing specific banking tycoons, politicians and un-convicted rapists in an attempt to make the world a better place. I asked him if he thought it was possible to make the world a better place by killing people. It was something I had been thinking about a lot at the time.

"Yes, I am sure of it. Actually, I think that killing bad people is good for your karma, and that if you do it then you will be rewarded," said Paul, and I looked into his eyes, and for the first time knew that I was in the car with a madman.

That night, after we had turned down the offer of travelling further with Jay and Paul, they set us down in a town called

Trofors. We hugged them both goodbye and watched the silver people carrier move away as they honked the horn and waved at us from the window. Once they had left, Imre turned to me and said, "So, are you a Nazi yet?"

We decided that before looking for a spot to camp we would go dumpster-diving. I had never done it in Norway, and I wanted Imre to show me the ropes. Trofors was only a small town, with one small co-op as its only supermarket. In one of its bins, we found something like fifty cakes and some cherries. We dug the best ones out, and then sat down to eat on a picnic table in a little park not far from the co-op. As we ate, we talked about the two Austrians. Imre said he was used to Nazis because they were common in Hungary, but what he found most distasteful was how Paul used Nordic and Germanic legend to suit their ideologies—and got it wrong. Apparently, a lot of Nazis do that. During the journey, Paul had told Imre that Hungarians had been "upgraded" to Austrians when the Austro-Hungarian Empire had been formed. Imre laughed as he told me this.

"And he believed that all the different races came from their own planet," Imre said. "But this is the black planet, the one we're on now. The gods moved us onto it."

"Why did they do that?"

"I don't know. But I don't think he was very happy with the decision. Did you like them?"

"Yeah," I said, "kind of."

"I did too; they were nice guys. But could you introduce him to your friends back in England?" he asked, and I told him that I didn't think I could.

There were a few different types of cakes, but my favourite one was more like a pastry, with a well in the middle filled with custard. I ate four, one after the other, and Imre did the same.

Once he had finished eating, Imre looked proudly at me and said, "This is the life." And I looked at my strange new friend and realised that for the first time in months I was actually happy.

The next morning, we found our way back to the E6 and got hitching again. According to Imre, the E6 ran the entire length of the country, and was the only road we'd need to take us to Nordkapp if we didn't want to make any diversions. Our first ride that day was with a father and son who were driving a converted minibus with a purple interior. The seats had big cushions on them, like a sofa. They were playing all the music I used to listen to as a teenager, stuff like Smashing Pumpkins and The Offspring. I loved it. I could tell that Imre was enjoying the music too. Towards the end of the journey, the son turned to us and asked what we thought of the Norwegian mountains, and we both said they were magnificent.

"Just wait 'til you see the mountains further north," he said, and smiled. His dad smiled at us too and said, "Yes, just wait."

One hundred kilometres later we reached Mo i Rana, which in England would have been a small town, but for that part of Norway was a substantial settlement, with residential areas and three big supermarkets. We went through the skips of each of the supermarkets and found another huge bag of cakes, along with fruit and sandwiches, which Imre wouldn't eat because they had meat in them and he was worried they'd make him sick. The town ran along the side of a fjord, and we walked by the water past a car park that had a seating area with picnic tables. On one of the tables, someone had left a half-finished bag of cheesy curls and we picked that up to add to our feast. Carrying our food, we walked towards the outskirts of the city to a park that was home to a wooden shelter with a bench and a table inside. We sat down and spread the food out on the table.

As we ate, we talked about the rides we'd had over the past two days. We played "Which race planet would you choose to live on if Paul's mystical beliefs were real," but the game fell apart when we couldn't decide the parameters for each planet. We weren't sure if South American Amazonian people would inhabit the same planet as Native Americans, and we were pretty sure there couldn't be a Pan-Asian planet, with both Chinese and South Asian Indian people living together; they just looked too different.

"I don't know what we should do with the Eskimos," Imre said, and so we gave up. "It doesn't matter anyway," he said, "I'd choose the white planet because what if the other people on the other planets turned out to be racists?" and I looked at his olive skin, moustache and little beard that looked like a Chinese monk's from a cartoon, and said, "Yeah, we'd let you in, but only because you were upgraded by the Austrians."

"I like when people here see you going through garbage near the supermarkets," he said. "They probably expect it of me, an Eastern European, but when they see you with blonde hair and blue eyes, you are doing a lot to break down social stereotypes."

That day we passed into the Arctic Circle, and as our lift had time to kill, he stopped the car and showed us the sights like a tour guide. The area was almost barren, with no trees and blunt little hills. There was a tourist centre and a modest piece of abstract art made from wood and shaped like a compass dial. There was also a plaque that marked the area as the start of the Arctic. Imre took out his tablet and got me to take a photo of him next to the artwork because some of his friends in Hungary didn't always believe him when he told them about the travelling he had done. He had decided to get some pictures as evidence this time. When Imre had finished, we were taken thirty kilometres further north where the trees thickened again, and our ride dropped us off outside a derelict timber mill.

Our next ride was a guy called Simon, who invited us back to his cabin, which was nestled in the woods, perhaps a mile from the E6. He offered us cheese from a tube with bread and wine. I refused the wine and liked that when I said I didn't drink or smoke anymore, both Simon and Imre didn't seem to make any judgments or even ask me any questions about it. Simon asked us about our trip and our lives back in our home countries. He had the best way of agreeing with you as you spoke: He would widen his eyes and nod his head almost frantically, like he was desperate for you to know that he was on your side. It was an expression completely without pretence, and I loved it.

Imre and I gave Simon an outline of our journey. I told Simon about my bus getting turned around at the Channel Tunnel due to a riot in the migrant refugee camps in Calais; and about Chris—an American guy who was the COO of a company that owned campsites in Southern Norway—who had put me up for a night, taken me out for a meal and even given me a pair of socks when he saw that mine were full of holes; all just out of the goodness of his heart. Imre and I compared the different countries we had passed through based on the ease of getting picked up: Denmark was the agreed upon top, and Imre said France was also very good. I found Germany and Norway to be about the same.

As he drank a few glasses of wine, Simon told us about his life. He had been a soldier in the King's Guard as part of his national service. He was on duty the day Anders Breivik bombed a government building in Oslo and then shot another

69 people at a socialist youth camp. Simon had spent that day running around Oslo—eighteen years old and with live ammunition—and then the three following nights sleeping in the King's garage in case of a secondary attack. He was also a member of Rød, a socialist Norwegian political party, and had just returned from Turkey, where he had been working with the Kurdish politicians during the election—because they thought the presence of Western people would dissuade corrupt officials from tampering with the voting booths. Simon was also at the Diyarbakır rally when the bomb went off. First, he heard the blast but couldn't see much; then people started emerging from a neighbouring street covered in blood and dust, with ripped-up clothes. After a while, Simon's voice trailed off, and Imre changed the subject.

We swapped stories about our friends who had gotten so drunk that they had pissed themselves, and talked about comedy we liked; then Simon told us about a time he was driving through one of Norway's many tunnels, and for some reason he could smell iron, and then when he got to the end of the tunnel, he passed a reindeer that had been crushed by a truck and spread across twenty feet of wall like a fly on a window.

After a few hours it was time to go, so we hugged Simon goodbye and left his cabin before walking for a few kilometres with our thumbs out, looking for a good spot. There were long periods without any cars at all, but eventually we got a lift with a young Latvian guy called Janis, who was driving an old black Volvo like a madman. He told us he would take us all the way to Bognes. From there, we would have to take a ferry across a small fjord to a town called Skarberget, where we could carry on along the E6 to keep heading north. As Janis drove, the scenery became more and more awe-inspiring, with the mountains growing asymmetrical, their sharp tops covered in snow. With the water and the mist, it felt like we were in a Tolkien novel. I said this to Imre, and he nodded in agreement.

"Valinor," he said.

When we reached Bognes we had to wait the better part of an hour for the ferry to arrive. We spent the time talking, with Imre telling me a bit more about his life. It seemed that his vagrant lifestyle stemmed largely from a hatred towards conformity and affluence. He told me that he had worked on a Christmas tree farm in Denmark a few years previously, where there were three tiers of trees: budget, medium and luxury. Every time he needed to piss, he would walk ten minutes to the luxury section so that he could piss on a tree more likely to be bought by a rich person. He was part of a group of Hungarians who were employed by the Christmas tree factory through a work agency. Most of his Danish colleagues he liked, but a few he detested.

"One of the Danish guys there was the biggest pig I've met in my life," Imre said. "The first time I met him, there was a group of us Hungarians sitting drinking beer, and he walked to us and didn't say anything. Instead, he just turned his back to us and took a piss, and he did a huge fart at the same time while pissing. When he was finished, he turned, put his hand out and just said 'Pevo' to us, because he doesn't think there's any difference between the Eastern European languages, and to him we're all just one undefined mass of Hollywood villains. There was also a young Danish girl who was extremely stupid. You know the type who expends effort into not learning? She was actually struggling to be stupid. But most of the other guys were nice. I liked my boss."

After the Christmas tree farm, Imre drifted between Hungary and hippie communes in Europe for a year before heading back to Denmark to work on a dairy farm. He'd found the job through the same agency he had used a year earlier, but this time he hated his boss, and all the other employees were exclusively Russian speaking. He walked out of the farm in the middle of the night after one of his shifts and didn't tell anyone he was leaving. He wanted to start his journey on foot and didn't want to carry his full rucksack with him, so he left most of his clothes and belongings in the accommodation provided by the farm. "I left all of my stuff there on my bed and floor. It was like I faked my death," he told me. He didn't even bother getting his wages before he left.

Imre didn't pry into my life, and I liked that. He didn't ask about my dad at all. On the few occasions that he asked about Rishni, my girlfriend, it felt like more of a formality; like the way you ask about someone's partner when you meet them for the first time at a dinner party. Imre was interested in Rishni's Indian heritage and wanted to know what language she spoke with her family, but that was it. He didn't want me to go into it, and I'd spent enough time over the previous five months turning the relationship over in my head that I didn't need to go over it all again, either. It would work out or it wouldn't.

The ferry arrived, and after we boarded, we started walking up to cars to see if someone would take us along the last leg to Narvik. But no one would even wind their window down to speak to us. They just shook their heads or pretended not to see us at all. We took turns asking because it was too demoralising for one person to take all the rejection.

We had absolutely no luck on board, so when the boat pulled into the port and the gate was opened, we ran to beat the cars onto the slipway. We stood to the side of the passing cars with our thumbs out. A young couple, who were in the last car to leave the ferry, stopped for us and said they could take us to Narvik. We got into the car quickly because we were blocking cars from boarding the ferry, and then Imre started giving the couple his usual introduction. I made up my mind that when we stopped, I was going to ask him not to do that at the start of every ride.

Narvik is a large fjordside town and a major port for the shipping of iron ore from Sweden. It was cold when we arrived, and I thought I could smell the sour, metallic odour of the iron ore in the air. We walked alongside the waterfront and found a supermarket with a bin filled with a hundred wheels of brie. We took as many of them as we could fit into our bags and then found a spot by the water, where we ate the brie on slices of fruitcake that we had found a day earlier. Once we had eaten, I dragged us around the town until we found a bank with an open Wi-Fi connection so that I could message Rishni. Imre took the opportunity to take out his tablet and check the university's grade boundaries.

"I got in!" he shouted, and then stood up and started pacing while roaring, "YES!" over and over again. I made some excuse about needing to piss and tried to find a shop that was open and serving alcohol so that I could buy him a beer for celebration, but everything was shut.

We found a Statoil and went in one at a time to use the bathroom to wash in. The cashier gave us both dirty looks as he watched us walk in with our rucksacks and hiking boots, but he didn't say anything. When we were both clean, we walked around the town for a long time looking for a bus stop for Imre to sleep in because it looked like it might rain. Eventually we found one on the outskirts of the city, and as there was nowhere to put my tent, I made my bed up in the bus stop beside him. As

I was going to sleep, I realised that I didn't notice the way Imre smelt anymore.

In the morning I woke up with a bus parked directly in front of me. It was the first night I had spent out of my tent, and I had found it hard to sleep because of the constant midnight sun. Imre was still sleeping, and I noticed he had covered his eyes with one of his shirts as he slept. I decided that I would try to do the same if I slept outside again.

Our first ride that day was with a businesswoman who talked a lot about how rich Norway was. Despite picking us up, she seemed to disapprove of us hitchhiking and was determined to help me book my flight home right there in the car using her mobile phone. I tried telling her that I didn't plan on going home for weeks, but she didn't want to listen to me. She seemed to think that I wouldn't be able to work out how a Norwegian website works.

"Us Norwegians work in a very particular way," she said while scrolling through the Norwegian flights website for me. "But it is because of this that we are also very naive; we don't know how other peoples do things. Such as when I went on holiday in Morocco, I was cheated all the time. We are just not used to it here in Norway, as people do not cheat one another here. Only now there are many immigrants changing Norway and making it a different place, and in many ways a dirtier place."

Probably to change the subject, Imre started talking to her about the pronunciation of Norwegian words. I noticed how he slowly seemed to have gained some understanding of the way the written language worked during the few days we had spent together. Then our host started talking a lot about how clean the air was in Norway.

"It's not as clean in our countries," Imre said, saying anything to make the atmosphere she was creating less weird. "That's why we're all getting cancer."

Before we could leave the car, she made me repeat the names of all the websites that offered cheap flights out of Norway to make sure I knew them. When she was confident I had remembered the websites she had shown me, she nodded and put her phone back into her pocket, and we got out of the car. As she drove away Imre said, "I hope I didn't say the wrong thing then, when I talked about cancer, because of your dad." But of course I didn't mind.

The further north we got the more the traffic thinned out and the more sheep we saw in the roads. We had long waits between rides, and we talked a lot. We talked about drinking a bit; Imre said that although he had done stupid stuff when he was drunk, it wasn't anything he wouldn't have done when he was sober. "I can't say I've done anything stupid or really bad *because* I was drunk," he said, and I told him that I had. "It's good that you stopped, then," he said.

"Do you ever speak to your parents when you travel?" I asked him as we waited.

"No, not at all. I recently stopped talking to my mum entirely."

"Oh, sorry, man. What about your dad?"

"He died when I was young," Imre said. I said I was sorry. "He was a good guy, I guess. I think he had something to do with the mafia. Or at least at his funeral, a mafia boss turned up and then his best friend ran away."

"What was his job?"

"He sold used cars. He drove around the country selling them. He was a good guy from what I can remember. People always say that it's sad because my dad is gone and I don't speak to my mum or brother anymore, but I don't think it is because my mum and brother are shitty people. I don't think that there's anything sad about not speaking to someone you don't like."

"Did you just not get on or was it one specific thing that you fell out over?" I asked.

"We argued a lot for years, but eventually it was just a normal argument that was the final straw. I told her to...it's hard to translate...we say it quite a lot in Hungary...I guess it means something like...eat my ass out?" And even though we were supposed to be having a serious conversation, I couldn't help but laugh. He started laughing too.

"Well, no wonder," I said.

"I still have people who care about me," he said. "I've got some really good friends, so it's really not that bad."

After a few hours of waiting, a caravan pulled up with a French number plate. A woman got out and said, "Bonjour," and Imre said, "Vous êtes française?" as excited as a child. He started speaking to her in French. He was so excited that he was shaking. We got into the back, and Imre talked to her through the gap between the seats. I could hear him introducing me. I found it infuriating that he hadn't even given me the chance to speak for myself. I listened to them speaking and could understand most of what was said, but I couldn't think of anything to say. I got frustrated and started to think that Imre was sneering at me: the English guy who can only speak English. Eventually I got pissed off and clumsily cut into their conversation to say that I like the wine in Bordeaux, which is where she was from. Imre had to help me get the message across, though, because my pronunciation was so bad. The woman seemed to like talking about wine, and she and Imre spoke intermittently about it for the rest of the journey. They also talked a lot about the

Norwegian scenery, particularly the mountains. During the quiet patches, Imre smiled that same lazy half-smile that he used while waiting for a ride, and it made me think about what an arrogant bastard he was. I decided that when we got out of the caravan I would tell him that I thought he was arrogant; but I fell asleep, and when it was time to leave the caravan I woke up confused, and by then had pretty much forgotten that I was angry with Imre.

The French lady dropped us off at a town called Nordkjosbotn, where the road split. She explained to Imre in French that she would be bearing northwest along the E8, until she reached Tromsø, which was the only sizable settlement in that part of Norway. We were to carry on along the E6 for another five or six hundred kilometres to Nordkapp. Imre and I discussed hitching straight away, but Imre thought we should check for food first.

"Maybe they have some good garbage here," he said, and the word *garbage* was drawn out and enjoyed, so that in his Hungarian accent it sounded almost like he was gargling with the word in the back of his throat. It was disgusting.

The first skip we opened was filled with frozen pizzas that we had no use for. We dug around until I unearthed a packet of ice cream sandwiches, which had been kept cold by the huge mound of semi-frozen pizzas around them.

"Are they fucking ice cream sandwiches?" Imre almost shouted, and he took the packet out of my hands and looked it over. "I've been seeing these advertised since I got into the country. This little Eskimo on the front is the brand logo. Are there any more?" We moved more of the pizzas out of the way to find maybe ten boxes buried. We took a box each and also some blueberries that were sitting on the far right, completely undamaged, probably also preserved by the cold from the frozen food.

We found a picnic bench and sat down. I took some bowls out of my rucksack and washed the blueberries using my bottle of water, and then we both filled our bowls with semi-melted ice cream sandwiches and sprinkled the blueberries on top.

"It's like when you're a kid and you go to a sweet shop, and you're only allowed a little bag," Imre said. "So you say that when you grow up, you're going to buy all the sweets in the shop, but you never actually do it. I've been seeing adverts for these ice cream sandwiches for nearly two weeks now. I kept on seeing this smug little Eskimo," and he pointed to the little smiling Inuit on the side of the box. He did look smug. "But I never had the money to buy any." Then he took a big triumphant spoonful of ice cream and said, "Who's smiling now, bitch?"

After eating the ice cream, we realised that the local Statoil hadn't locked its skip. Imre walked over to check it out but got caught in the act by one of the employees who had come to dump some rubbish. Imre hurried back over to me, embarrassed. "We should come back later; there were loads of cakes and sandwiches in there," he said. "There were so many that I was sorting out the good and bad ones because I couldn't carry all of them."

We ended up returning to the town again that night, after a few hours standing on the outskirts not getting lifts. But when we went back to the Statoil skip, someone had poured what looked like old coffee granules and water over the bag of cakes so that we couldn't eat them.

"Fucking asshole," Imre said. "It must have been that guy who saw me earlier. I knew he was going to do something like that." Then he went to use the toilet in the garage. Because we had almost no food left, I bought some crackers and cheese, and made a little picnic up as a surprise. I spread the food out on the grass behind the garage. A few minutes later, Imre came and sat down opposite me. We both started eating in silence for a while.

"Did you buy this stuff?" he asked, eventually.

When I told him that I had, he said, "Well, thank you for buying unnecessary shit I could have shoplifted."

The hitch from Nordkjosbotn to Alta took three days, and we spent hours standing on the side of the road at long-forgotten bus stops waiting for rides or walking along the abandoned E6 looking for "a better spot." The weather got colder as we got further north, and Imre would get grumpy at the end of every day when the traffic started drying up. We always seemed to end the day miles away from the nearest town, a long way from any shelter, which meant that if we didn't get a ride, Imre would have to sleep out in the open since he didn't have a tent. A few times I suggested that should that situation arise, he could squeeze into my tiny one-man tent. He always dismissed the offer. I suspected that he'd sooner die of exposure than accept that bringing a tent was a good idea.

The atmosphere soured further when a van heading in the opposite direction stopped, and an old man leant out the window to tell us there had been an avalanche ten kilometres up the road, meaning that we would be unable to get any further. He said we would have to turn around and head to a town called Lyngseidet, where we could take a ferry across the fjord and rejoin the E6 further north. We thanked the old man and then sat down next to a roadside supermarket, where Imre looked at the map on my phone and I looked through the supermarket bins for food. All I found that was edible were a couple of red peppers going brown in places. I cut the bad bits out with my penknife and ate the rest while Imre showed me the route he thought we could take.

"Or I was thinking maybe we could just walk it?" Imre said once he had shown me all other possible options.

I agreed, as I didn't want to end up back in Nordkjosbotn, where we both felt we had slowly outstayed our welcome. But then a few kilometres into our walk another car stopped, and the woman driving told us that she had just seen the rockslide. She said that rocks were still falling, and it would be too dangerous to even try and pass on foot. We turned around and started hitching back the way we had come.

We walked with our thumbs out and at first saw no cars for a long time; then after half an hour or so, two young guys in an old muscle car drove up slowly behind us and stopped. An air freshener the shape of a pine tree but in the colours of the American flag hung in the windscreen. We pulled our bags tighter onto our shoulders and ran over to the car, but just as we reached them, they pulled away and sped off, laughing out the window at us as they went. We started walking again. Over the course of the evening they did it to us two more times, and we fell for it every time. After the third time I filled my pockets with projectiles—stones from the side of the road, a broken lighter, a metal bolt—just in case they passed us again.

As the waits between rides lengthened, Imre and I started bickering. I still hadn't properly forgiven him for the way he had arrogantly smiled when speaking to the French lady a day earlier, and the mood grew more tense with every car that passed us. Twice, cars with British number plates passed us without stopping. When the second one passed, Imre mentioned this, and I said the cars looked pretty full.

"The Austrians who didn't have space stopped for us and the French who didn't have space stopped for us," he said. "The British cars just drive past."

"Yeah, well, who knows," I said. "Maybe they're just arse-holes. It's not common to hitchhike in the UK. A bunch of Polish cars have passed us and didn't stop, and you didn't mention them."

"But I love Polish people. In fact, I hope they take over the whole of the UK."

"You haven't even been to the UK. Maybe you'd like it the way it is."

"I don't want to. I don't think I'd like it."

"But Imre, you haven't even been—how do you know?"

"Generally, my preconceptions of a place are right. They've always been right so far."

"It's one of the most populated and diverse countries in Europe. It probably *is* the most diverse country in Europe, and London is the biggest city in the European Union. I'm sure you could find something you like there."

"I'd rather live in Oslo or Helsinki than in London."

"OK, but there is more happening in London than in either of those places, so I refuse to believe that you could go to London and not, in some way, enjoy your time."

"You only need so much. You have everything you need in Helsinki. I'd hate to go to London."

"You have everything you need in fucking Nordkjosbotn," I said. "But I wouldn't want to live there." Both of us had started raising our voices.

"They earn so much in Norway you could probably live in Oslo and fly to any city you want on the weekend," said Imre.

29

"Yes, but...this argument is absurd. I don't even like London."

"I'd rather live in *that* house than in London!" Imre nearly shouted, and he pointed to a little wooden house that was falling apart on the side of the road. "Or maybe I could live in one of the Polish areas in London. I like Polish people."

"I like Polish people too," I said. "They do a great job with our manual labour." I hated myself as soon as I said it. "I didn't mean that," I said, my voice panicky. I could tell that I had shocked Imre. I was shocked too. "I do the same jobs as most Polish immigrants! They've been my colleagues everywhere I've worked. Some of them are my good friends!"

"That's what all the racists say—that they've got black friends, or whatever."

We waited for well over two hours but finally got a ride with a glamorous twenty-four-year-old primary school teacher, who played trance music as she drove us halfway to the ferry in Lyngseidet. She told us that she had spent time teaching in South Africa, and made every possible effort to pick up hitchhikers. After she'd dropped us off, Imre said, "Well, I'm in love, are you in love?" Then we waited half an hour before being picked up by another young woman, who was also beautiful but very chubby, and she took us all the way to the ferry and also paid for our ferry tickets. She was called Astrid.

Once on the ferry, the three of us headed to the ferry canteen, where we talked and drank coffee. Astrid said she worked with people with learning difficulties and autism, and had a very rich father who owned a big salmon factory. She drove a brand-new BMW 4x4 and kept referring to us both as her "two lucky charms" because she too had been held up by the avalanche and was hoping for more luck in the next leg of her journey home. She told us that she hated killing animals but didn't mind working in her dad's salmon factory. Apparently, the factory workers used a special device that pumped cold water towards the salmon. This made the salmon instinctively swim towards the flow of the water, which led them into the arms of some machine that would stun them and slit their throats.

"It's an active suicide for the salmon, so I can't feel bad," she said.

When the boat pulled into the port we walked from the canteen, climbed into Astrid's car, disembarked the ferry and rejoined the road. A short while later it was time for Astrid to head east, and she wished us luck and left us at the roadside. We started making our way north through a string of short, broken-up rides with locals who were driving to and from work, relatives' houses or their local supermarket. As we moved deeper into the Arctic, the forests grew thinner until they disappeared almost entirely. Sometimes the mountain range would form a valley with patches of woods, but the thick forests that were everywhere in the south were gone. The absence of trees meant clear views of the mountains, which were covered in bristly grass or sometimes just plain stone: colossal walls of rock that rose up like approaching waves as you travelled towards them. Small chunks of the same stone were underfoot whenever we were left by the roadside—green-grey strips of rock with veins of white in little flat shards; almost like slate, but thicker. Every now and then we'd pass patches of a handful of wooden cabins like Simon's, which were always painted the colour of rust.

We made it to Alta the following evening. Two rides got us there. The first driver was half Sámi, with dark eyes but the milk-white skin of a southern Norwegian. He was driving his sister's car home to do some repairs on it.

"What's wrong with the car?" I asked him, looking ahead at the road, which followed the side of the mountain, with just a flimsy metal fence running alongside as a barrier. "I hope it's not the brakes," I joked.

"Actually," he said as we were passing a cliff edge with a two-hundred-foot drop, "it is."

The second driver was John, who drove us the full four hours to Alta. When we got into his car, John was listening to a cover of Tom Waits's *Chocolate Jesus* that I had never heard before. John was a carpenter, middle-aged and hungover. He smoked constantly as he drove, and his chin, which he scratched before answering a question, was covered with a few days' stubble. John reminded me of a cowboy. He told us about a time he was drunk and had borrowed his friend's motorbike and crashed it. John was out of work for three years with the injuries. He lived well during those three years; the Norwegian government really took care of him. They even paid for him to do a degree from home.

Towards the end of the journey, John told us about his job. He travelled around a few different towns fixing houses on behalf of the government.

"The immigrants living in the houses I fix," he said, "you wouldn't believe the stuff that they break. The owners of the houses don't even charge the immigrants themselves; can you imagine billing them? Mohammed...Akbar...no one even knows who they are. We just go to the government, and they pay the bill for them."

In Alta, John dropped us off outside a REMA 1000, and we found hundreds of kilos of nuts in the bins. We also found some really sweet biscuits and some chocolate sauce for filling pastries. We sat down on a wooden crate next to the supermarket, and I pretended to be a waiter in a restaurant serving Imre.

"So, good sir, what can I get for you today?"

"Well, what do you have?"

"Umm, well, we have nuts and biscuits, and...nuts and biscuits and some weird chocolate shit we can spread on top of the nuts and biscuits."

"What do you recommend?"

"I personally recommend the nuts and biscuits with the chocolate shit spread on top."

"Then I guess I'll go for the nuts and biscuits with that stuff on top."

"An excellent choice."

We moved on from Alta that day, spending the night camping next to a school in a small rural town, with Imre in the bus stop sheltering from the rain that was coming down heavily. In the morning, when I was looking for a tap to fill my water bottle with, a woman working in the school noticed me and came out to offer us both a shower in the school gym. She had seen us sleeping by the entrance when she arrived that morning. We took the shower gratefully, and before we left she said we could use the shower again if we came back the same way.

We got to Nordkapp that day. First, we travelled with three women driving a brand-new sports car that the eldest said she had won in a radio show competition, and then a Lithuanian couple drove us the rest of the way. We passed herds of reindeer, and as we got closer to Nordkapp, the trees in the little patches of woodlands got smaller, shrinking in size and thinning out, and then stopped appearing altogether. We got out of the car and walked the last five hundred metres—because to enter the North Cape itself you had to pay for each passenger in the car; but if you walked on foot, you didn't pay anything. It was midnight when we got there. The sun was still up, but it was low enough to have yellowed the sky slightly, like the start of a sunset.

Nordkapp was OK. It had a good view of the ocean, but it was filled with tourists. The ground was brown dirt, tired and stamped completely flat by a million holidaymakers. The earth stretched out towards the water until it reached the cliff edge. Three hundred feet below, the ocean threw itself against grey rock. There was a metal fence marking the perimeter of the cliff and a café filled with German families eating sandwiches that cost more than £15 each. Up until then, all the water we'd seen had been in fjords. In comparison to the fjords, the sea at Nordkapp seemed so vast it was intimidating. It did kind of feel like the end of the world.

We took a few photos of us leaning against the metal fence, with the midnight sun behind us, and then went into the tourist office to use the Internet and charge our phones. Other tourists stared at us as we sat on the floor. They could probably smell us. I watched Imre as he used his tablet; he was smiling the same distant smile, and I decided that it was probably just involuntary rather than arrogant. When our phones were charged, we started walking south again on foot. Imre had read online about a community cabin that was left open overnight in a town fifteen kilometres from Nordkapp. We got a lift after just a few minutes of walking, without even putting our thumbs out. Our ride took us straight to the cabin, which was right next to the water in a little bay. In the morning, I woke up and walked onto the beach and saw whales breaching in the cove.

Imre and I parted ways that day. We hitched together to

Honningsvåg, and before we got out of the car, the guy driving us said, "Can I offer you two some advice? Take a shower and wash your clothes." We then walked to the REMA 1000, where we found two very good loaves of bread in the bin. I went into the shop and bought some brown cheese and two of the cakes with the custard filling that we had eaten the first time we camped together. We sat together and ate some of the bread and cheese, and then we divided the rest of the food between us.

We walked together to the outskirts of the town, where I had seen a youth hostel signposted. Imre was looking for a spot to hitch from; when none appeared, he said, "I might just use this bend here," and pointed to a bend where the road widened slightly. I was turning left there anyway.

"We have each other's email addresses," I said. "Make sure you contact me if you ever come to England."

"Yeah, and you too, if you ever come to Hungary."

I went to shake his hand, but Imre put his arms out and we hugged awkwardly. We were tired, and our arguments from the previous days were still around us.

"Take care on your hitch home," I said. "Good luck with your degree."

"And you. I hope everything goes OK with your dad."

"Thanks."

Then we parted ways. When I got to the hostel, I had a long shower and washed all my clothes. The next day I started hitching south from that same bend, but by then Imre was long gone.

2

Dexterity

The Walk to Spain—One

In the night the storm had pulled down trees around South West England. I was camping in Noss Creek, in South Devon, trying to sleep on a roll mat and a sleeping bag in a huge family tent, all of which I'd stolen a few weeks before while drunk. The camping was practice because I was due to start my walk to Spain in two weeks' time, which would mean a lot of camping alone, and camping alone had always gone badly for me.

The sides of my stolen tent were nearly six feet tall. As the storm picked up, the tent caught the wind like a sail, with the wall of it blowing flat against me every time the wind hit. As the night wore on, the wind grew stronger, and with each gust the fabric flapped against me, and the rain leached through the polyester wall into my sleeping bag. In the early hours of the morning, I decided that the tent poles were probably due to snap soon, and if that happened, I would be soaked by the rain almost immediately. And then who knew what would happen to me?

I put my waterproofs on and climbed out of the tent. My body weight must have been holding the tent down because when I stepped outside, it was blown two feet towards the creek. Worst of all, it had all my new gear inside. Gear I'd just spent four hundred quid on. I managed to grab hold of the fabric door but as I worked to anchor the tent down, it twisted, and the wind blew in through the open door and filled the tent like a balloon. It blew around frantically and I had to grip the sodden material with all my might so it didn't get wrenched out of my hands. Eventually, I managed to force the tent to the ground and held it down with my feet while I took the poles out; when this was done I lay on top, covering it with my whole body, reaching through the door like it was a sack, pulling out what was inside, one item at a time, so that I could pack it all into my backpack.

The fastest route out of Noss Creek started with a steep, muddy bank that my brother and I used to play on when we were kids. The only way to get up the bank was to run up it at full speed and grab hold of a tree that stuck out at a forty-five-degree angle halfway up. From there I could pull myself up using the branches of neighbouring trees. I held my stolen roll mat to my chest and started up the hill as fast as I could, but quickly lost my momentum; I was soon reduced to taking heavy, plodding steps with my legs spread wide, trying to keep my feet steady in the mud. After a few metres, both of my feet went out from under me, and I fell. I fell so quickly it was as if the ground had been pulled out backwards while I stood on it, and I was propelled into the wet soil and grit. As I dropped to the ground my roll mat landed upright in front of me on the bank, and my face made full contact with the other end of it. My head jolted back on impact and pain shot through my neck. With my nose and neck ringing, I slid to the bottom of the hill, as wet and helpless as a newborn lamb. It took five more attempts before I managed to take hold of the tree, climb to the top of the bank and start the walk home.

The day I left for Spain, I woke up at seven in the morning and ate the breakfast my dad had cooked for me. He pottered around the kitchen as I ate. The corrupted cell that would later become a tumour was probably already inside his chest that morning, but if you'd told me that at the time, I would never have believed you: my dad was slim and fit for his age and had given up smoking years earlier. In his fifties he moved around the kitchen like a man in his thirties. He still had the air of indestructibility I attributed to him when I was a child.

After eating, I went back to my room and opened a card I had been given by my brother, Jack. In the card, he had written:

Make sure you take all the good advice that you have given to me over the years.

I put the card into my diary, which in turn I put into a waterproof plastic bookbag next to several books I was taking. I wore a Māori necklace that my sister had worn the whole time she had been travelling and had passed on to me for good luck.

I shouldered my bags and Dad took the family dog, Monty, and together we walked towards the Devon coast until we reached Little Dartmouth. It was nearing the end of January, and the sky was marbled with white-grey clouds; the air was remorseless and cold. When we reached the wooden gate marking the start of the next parish, Dad said it was time for him to head home, back to the village where I had spent the first nineteen years of my life and where he and my mother still lived. We hugged and he told me to look after myself, calling me "Son." I could tell by his voice that he was working hard not to cry. He started back along the path from where we had just come, and I continued the walk west, stopping after a few metres to watch him walk away, even though I knew it would make me feel wretched.

When Dad was out of view, I began to make my way along the South West Coast Path, which is nearly seven hundred miles of hard, winding trail originally forged by coastguards who walked it looking for smugglers. It passes by every cove and bay the coastline has to offer in the South West of the country; anywhere smugglers could have landed a boat to bring in goods illegally. The Coast Path connects my parents' house to Plymouth, and following it was easy; I just had to make sure the sea was on my left. Once I'd accounted for the detours to every little beach, I worked out that I would be on the Coast Path for around seventy miles. Then, from Plymouth, I would be able to take a ferry to France.

Once in France I planned to start heading south towards Spain. From the Spanish border I would follow the Camino de Santiago across Spain itself. The Camino is an ancient pilgrimage that runs to a holy Catholic site in Santiago de Compostela; originally it had belonged to the druids and led all the way to the west of Spain, to Cape Finisterre. I thought I might follow the druid path as long as I had time.

As I walked, a cold wind came in from the sea and hit me so that I had to screw up my eyes to protect them. The Coast Path rose and fell frequently, with sharp climbs followed by sharp descents. I was carrying two bags: one big rucksack and one shoulder bag, which was filled almost entirely with food. I didn't know it then, but the Coast Path would actually end up being the hardest part of the whole walk.

On that first day I set out to travel about twelve miles. I passed through Blackpool Sands and Slapton Sands, two beaches that seemed to go on forever. Pebble and sand stretched out before me, imposing and incredible, like a giant washed-up spinal column. In school we had learnt how during the Second World War a whole platoon of American soldiers had been killed in a training exercise on Slapton Sands. In a freak accident, blank ammunition had been swapped with live shells, and the soldiers were gunned down as they landed on the beach. I thought about the young men dying as I walked; and in the bad weather and in my solitude, it was easy to believe that all those young men had died right there.

At the end of the beach, I sat down next to a war memorial to eat. As I un-popped the catch on my rucksack, I could feel the blood flowing back into the tissue on my shoulders. After the disaster at Noss Creek, I had replaced my chunky family gear with a lightweight mountaineering tent and a small inflatable roll mat, but I still had too much to carry. My dad had packed me canned fish, fruit and some dried food, but the shoulder bag still pulled at my neck like a noose. I made up my mind to eat as much of it as quickly as possible so that I would be able to get rid of the second bag entirely. As I ate, I felt pleased with my circumstances despite the discomfort. I had a rare feeling of certainty about the choices I was making.

I planned to carry on walking for another two hours, but it ended up being almost twice that, as finding a place to camp on the Coast Path was almost impossible. The ground was uneven and craggy, and when I did find somewhere that wasn't a cliff edge, I couldn't get my pegs into the rocky earth. Occasionally, I passed areas of squat woodlands or little patches of grass, but even in these areas the ground was composed of just a few centimetres of soil before becoming solid rock. My tent was designed to be as light as possible, meaning that it had only one pole to support its shape and relied on the anchorage from the pegs to keep it up. I'd get one peg in, then spend a precious ten minutes walking around trying to find another patch of soft earth for the next one, before being forced to accept defeat, packing up again and trying to find another spot. With the light fading, I grew desperate and hopped over a dry stone wall, pitching up on what looked like the back of somebody's lawn, planning to get out early the next day before anyone noticed I was there. From inside my tent, I could hear construction work being done on a neighbouring house. The work carried on late into the evening, and I listened to one of the workers whistling as I lay in my sleeping bag.

I already had blisters on both my feet, and as I lay there before sleeping, I could feel them throbbing, and my legs and shoulders were also throbbing. My face, which was the only part of my body that wasn't covered by the sleeping bag, was so cold that my nose kept running. I was worried that I was going to get moved on or arrested for trespassing, but I still managed to slip into sleep better than I ever could at home. I slept straight through the night without waking once. In fact, I slept so well that when I woke up in the morning, I felt vulnerable in my little tent: If anyone had visited me as I slept, I wouldn't have known anything about it.

I was amazed by the speed at which my feet began to disintegrate. By lunchtime on my second day, the blisters on my feet had grown to two inches wide and had filled with a creamy, yellow fluid. The pain of walking with the blisters put me in a foul mood. I pierced one blister that was on the side of my heel with my penknife, which gave me some relief, but I couldn't find it in me to puncture the ones directly on the soles of my feet.

They burned as I walked, forcing me to hobble as I moved. The tourists eating in the local pubs stared at me as I passed because of the way I was walking. My movement had regressed from a limp through to a waddle, and by the time I reached Salcombe, I was walking like I had shit myself. On a few occasions people stopped their car next to me and offered me a lift, and each time I could tell that they were worried about me. I refused every offer, pissed off, and trudged into Salcombe, hobbling like Quasimodo despite the fact I'd only walked thirty miles.

I spent the night in a walkers' hostel, where the man working in reception voiced all his thoughts, laughing vacantly after each sentence, looking me in the eye the whole time.

"How much veg is in the vegetarian curry? Ho ho ho. Does he have enough change in his wallet to cover it? Ha ha."

I couldn't tolerate him.

The day after Salcombe, the Coast Path led me through fields that despite the time of year, were vibrant green with small, rubbery stems sprouting out of the dark earth. I couldn't identify the species. They looked more like the stems of flowers than a farm crop. Between the low, green plants, the path stretched into the distance. Briefly, the clouds broke just enough overhead to let through a few brilliant rays of sunshine, illuminating my path like a piece of religious artwork.

The day was further improved when I made a conscious effort to eat all the heavy food in the shoulder bag. Along with the food items, my dad had also given me a small plastic chessboard, which he hoped might help me transcend language barriers in rural France. He'd also given me a length of thick electrical cable he called a "cosh" that he used to take for self-defence when fishing in an area known for attracting poachers. I made space for these two items in my rucksack. There was also a spare torch and a spare can opener, which, when all the food was gone, I pushed into the bin followed by the shoulder bag itself. I felt guilty as I did it, thinking of my dad preparing it all for me, but practicalities came first. That night I pitched up in a field just under twenty miles from Plymouth, behind a dry stone wall that bore the brunt of the wind tearing in from the sea.

The next day I got moving early in the morning, despite my ruined feet. I passed by fields that were home to scattered flocks of sheep grazing on pale-green grass wet with the melting frost. I occasionally passed trees that had lost their leaves to winter—tangled, brown statues contorted by the constant wind coming in from across the water. Smaller, dead, brown plants were bunched on either side of the path. The fields were on my right-hand side. On my left was a constant sheer drop that made the base of my stomach feel like it was floating when I got close to it. Grey rocks the shape of teeth stuck out of the water, which foamed white as it broke around them.

By lunchtime of my fourth day on the road, I had reached the River Plym. The mouth of the Plym, which opens into the sea, was half a mile wide, so I was forced to turn inland, through five miles of thick woodlands and undulating hills. The footpath slowly became a small country road, and by late afternoon I could tell I was getting close to Plymouth: the patches of houses began to thicken, and the road I was on fed into a dual carriageway in the same way a stream feeds into a river. On the outskirts of the city, I found a supermarket, where I washed in the bathroom and bought six pairs of thick workman's socks, along with a small feast of meats, pastries and fruit. Outside the shop I sat on the ground with my back against the supermarket wall, cleaning my feet, redressing my blisters and eating packaged salami with my bare hands. People walking into the shop stared at me like I was scum, but I didn't care at all. When I was finished, I packed my stuff back into my bag and started walking again.

As I closed in on the harbour I began to march. The ferry from Plymouth would mark the end of my time in England and the end of my time on the Coast Path. As I moved through the shops and the tangle of people, I built up steam. The socks had done what I had hoped they would, padding my feet tighter into my boots so they rubbed less. My feet felt almost comfortable as I strode towards the harbour, and when I passed a homeless man, I gave him what I had left of my English currency; around twenty quid. I told him I wouldn't be needing it on the continent. I cut through the rest of the city without stopping once.

It was just getting dark when I arrived at the port, and I was struck by the emptiness of the place. There were no cars or people anywhere. I followed the signs to the ferries until I heard a voice shouting, "Excuse me!" From across the concrete port, I made out a man in a yellow high-vis jacket moving towards me. He was overweight. He hurried over to me in a gait that was somewhere between a walk and a run, yelling in a thick Irish accent as he went. "Excuse me, what are you doing here?" he shouted again, his voice rebounding on the empty concrete. "Are you lost?" When he got to me, he was out of breath.

"I'm trying to find the ticket office."

"Oh no, I'm sorry, but it's the servicing period now."

"What's that?"

"When we service the ferries. We do it every year. There's no ferries for ten days."

I refused to go home. My dad offered to come and get me and

then to drop me back at the port when the ferries had started running again, but I wouldn't do it. The round trip would have only taken an hour and a half, but to me that would have meant walking back to Plymouth when it was time to return. A lift was out of the question, and I knew I couldn't face the Coast Path again. My dad couldn't understand it, but it just wasn't an option. It had to be all in one go.

I spent the first night in a filthy hostel that housed a handful of vulnerable men on hard times, drinking Kronenbourg Export and watching a documentary on sharks; then, to save money, I moved on from the hostel and couch-surfed for a night. The following day I tracked down a childhood friend who put me up until the ferries started running again.

I also made a trip to the doctor, who told me that I had caused an infection in my foot by piercing a blister with a dirty knife and then sealing it with a plaster. A short course of antibiotics would sort it out. Apparently, the key was to keep the blister open once pierced to let it dry out; if I had kept it dry, my body probably could have taken care of the rest.

3

Pay and Dive Immediately

Sudan to Kenya—One

We sat around a campfire in Stafford eating barbeque sausage next to George's truck. George and Stephen drank beer and we passed a spliff between us. Stephen was George's cousin and a few years earlier had done almost the same trip George and I were planning, but he had travelled by motorbike rather than in a truck. Stephen and a friend had started in England and travelled south through Europe, then took the ferry from Greece to Libya. From Libya they headed east to Egypt before moving southwards through the rest of the continent. By 2015, a lot of this route was off limits for me and George: after the civil war, Libya was effectively a failed state with spiralling violence; Egypt was also in political turmoil and had started charging insane import fees for any vehicle brought into the country, effectively pricing us out. We were looking at Sudan as the most logical starting point.

You could still hear the traces of Stephens's South African childhood in his accent when he spoke, but the rolling Rs and stretched-out vowels had softened. He was enthusiastic about our trip. He was sure it was going to blow our minds.

"Especially you, Jay," Stephen said. "George, with your job, you're a pretty well-travelled man, but have you travelled that much, Jay?"

"Mainly in Europe, really," I said.

"Well, Jay has walked to Spain," said George, who seemed to have sunken into his coat after the pot and the beer.

"Jesus. On your own?" asked Stephen.

"Yeah, on my own," I said.

"Down France or what?"

"Yeah. Along England and down France."

"Jesus. Well at least for this one you've got some company."

"You're right, although I quite like being on my own nowadays."

"Yeah? Well, don't go Forrest Gumping it on this trip, anyway. Africa is a little bit more dangerous than France. I wouldn't recommend walking across it," said Stephen.

We had a few more drinks and the night drew to a close. The barbeque, which George and Stephen called a braai, was invisible in the dark. You could just see a small puddle of dulling embers.

"This is the thing," Stephen said, pointing at us with his index and middle finger, holding the spliff tucked between the two. "Driving across Africa is serious shit. Trust me mate, I was shitting myself before I went. And you're gonna be scared. That's natural. But this is the thing—George, if you die, it's *your* fault; Jay, if *you* die, it's George's fault. It was his idea and it's his truck."

———

47

If you're flying into Sudan, you have to go through Egypt; you can't fly there any other way. We were to go from London to Cairo and then from Cairo to Khartoum. In the airport in London, George gave me his phone so that I could add my Google account to it because I didn't own a smartphone. The Google logo unfolded and refolded itself as my emails uploaded. George and I drank coffee while talking about the trip and what we were leaving behind. I had only been with Rishni for two years, and we were planning to spend nearly a year apart. It was going to be difficult. This was the first functional relationship I'd been in, and I was determined not to make a mess of it like I had with all the others. For the first time in my life, I was with someone who I couldn't imagine life without.

George is two years older than me and I have known him all my life. Our mothers had met while in hospital together when pregnant with our older sisters. George had trained as a cadet in the Royal Fleet Auxiliary and at the time leading up to our trip was piloting private yachts. He'd worked hard and done well for himself, buying several houses around South West England that he rented out. He'd even bought and shipped our truck to Sudan on his own. This trip was his brainchild and was supposed to be one last hurrah before he had a go at settling down. I had organised all the visas; he had done most of the organisation for the vehicle.

George was definitely leading things, but it didn't seem to be getting to him. As we sat in Heathrow Airport he was like he had always been: confident to the point of cocksure; bossy but well-meaning. I had faith in him.

The prospect of going to Sudan terrified me. It terrified my parents too. It had only been a few years since the predominantly Christian South Sudan had gained independence from the North, which was predominantly Muslim. The separation followed twenty-two years of civil war; national wounds were still healing, and another civil war was still ongoing in the western region of Darfur. We were sticking to the east of the country, which was peaceful but under the control of President Omar al-Bashir, who was known to sympathise with Islamic extremists and who, in the 1990s, had even offered refuge to Osama bin Laden. In preparation for our time in Sudan, I had bought a travel guide for the country. There was only one on the market, and it had taken a long time to arrive. When it did, I opened it to discover that the entire first chapter was a summary of the kidnapping that had occurred in the country over the past decade.

I was scared by the prospect of Africa as a whole. Other than a short trip to Tunisia five years before, everything I'd done had been in Europe. George had made regular trips to South Africa and Namibia, and he was an experienced driver. He'd driven in a few developing countries, including South Africa, and had taken the same truck we were taking to Sudan on a trip across Morocco for a test run. I, on the other hand, had only passed my driving test the month before our flight was due and hadn't sat behind a wheel since. George told me not to worry about it, and that he thought my driving was good enough even if I didn't. It helped.

The flight to Cairo was like any other flight, and Cairo itself could have been Luton with a few more exotic plants, but the next leg to Sudan was noticeably different. The aeroplane was small and felt like it was made of material not thick enough for purpose. I told George I'd read that all Sudanese air services had been banned in Europe for safety reasons, and when we hit turbulence an hour in, I thought that even the air hostess looked uneasy. But the food was exceptional: well-seasoned meat and veg dishes, with spiced curds and whey for dessert. And the turbulence died down after a while.

When we landed in Khartoum there was a group of men crowded at the baggage collection. I was told by a man in a police uniform to go to a side room, which had five men in it. One of them went through all of my luggage while the other four stood in a crowd around me peering over each other's shoulders to look at what was in my bags. Every one of them was hassling me for money. They shook their hands in the air in a way Europeans do not, and they spoke in short bursts of jumbled English with heavy accents. They scared me. They kept repeating the word 'money' and putting their hands out. When my saxophone case appeared, they asked me to open it, and when I did they looked the instrument over and mimed playing the sax and laughed. I laughed too. A hand patted me on the back. Eventually, they finished examining my bag and were seemingly satisfied, and when they asked for money again it was said more gently than before. I gave one man a ten-dollar bill. A few of the other guys got excited and asked for money a final time, but I made out like it was all I had and started to collect my stuff. Another hand patted me on the back. As I walked out, I saw that George was in another identical little room, but the door was closed and a soldier stood in front of it. Out of ideas, I walked outside without him and waited, standing in the Sudanese sun, which was hot as hell.

The airport officials had taken George's camera, along with the two hard drives he kept alongside it. I knew something was wrong when George came out to meet me. His face was composed but he didn't look at me and he lit a cigarette straight away. We took a taxi to the hotel, and after we'd checked in, we called Ateef, the importer who was helping get the truck into Sudan. Ateef said he thought he'd be able to get our equipment back.

An hour or so later a very large man arrived at the hotel to give us a sim card for a Sudanese phone network. He was probably six foot five, broad shouldered, and had dark brown skin. He introduced himself as Ismail, and we shook his giant hand. He said that he worked for Ateef and that they would call us on the new sim card if they made any progress in retrieving our camera.

George's truck was to arrive in Port Sudan, but Ateef lived and worked in Khartoum, the capital and biggest city in Sudan. It was hard to say what exactly Ateef was doing for us, or if we needed him at all. We'd had a string of confused conversations with him over email when planning our flights, and it seemed like it was another company based in Port Sudan that was actually collecting the truck from the ship. But we had no other option; Ateef was the only Sudanese importer we could find online and the one who had put us in contact with the firm in Port Sudan. If nothing else, Ateef felt like a cultural translator, which seemed like a worthy investment in itself.

After Ismail left, I went out to buy some food from a neighbouring shop. It was only a short distance away, but the pavement was covered with an inch of sand, which made my feet lose traction with every step. Five steps felt like twenty. As I walked, all the people I passed greeted me in English and smiled. The shop itself was more of a marquee with a fabric roof. I bought some fruit, flatbread and vacuum-packed beef sausages. The man behind the counter was overweight.

"You like it here in Sudan?" he asked.

"Yeah."

"And the weather?"

"The weather is very good."

"You like it now, but in a week, you will hate it."

The truck was set to arrive in Port Sudan ten days following our arrival in Khartoum, and then it would have to clear customs, which we were told might take a few days on top of that. We planned to stay in Khartoum for something like a week before heading down to Port Sudan to collect it. That way we'd get to see the city. We needed to get our visas validated in a government office anyway, which everyone said could take a while. The hotel we were staying in was clean, and the staff spoke good English and were extremely friendly.

The first night we went to bed early, spending just a few hours talking to other European tourists who all said that the people they had met in Sudan were always very kind and helpful and that on the whole the country had been a pleasant one to travel in. The next day we woke late and spent what remained of the day mooching around the city, which was hotter than anywhere I'd ever been and had an unplanned feeling about it—places seemed to pop up where they happened to be built, not through design. You could walk for miles without a shop anywhere, and the pavement would sometimes vanish for no good reason, forcing you onto the road, and then reappear around the corner. There were no parks to speak of, but the cafés and shisha bars and restaurants did good trade, and at each street corner women sold tea and coffee from portable cupboards lined with little glass cups and little jars containing the different teas. Around them were a few seats where you could sit and drink your coffee while watching the local guys on the hectic streets socialising, doing business and praying.

———

On our second day, Ateef came to take us out. He had Ismail with him, as well as a young woman called Hiba, dressed all in red, and another man who called himself Nasif. In the two days we had spent in the country, we learnt that in Sudan you shake hands in a specific way: First you slap their left shoulder, then you shake their right hand. Greetings were a big deal. We greeted each of them in English and Arabic and shook everyone's hands in the Sudanese way, other than Hiba, whom we greeted verbally and with a smile. We also gave Ateef some English biscuits in an ornate tin we had bought at Heathrow Airport.

Ateef said he would like to take us to a café that was "European-style," so George and I walked to the road outside the hotel and climbed into a plush, air-conditioned 4x4 with Nasif, Ateef and Hiba, while Ismail followed in a brown Škoda. When we got to the coffee shop, we all sat down and Ateef asked us if we liked the interior, which was made up with dark red fabric and dark wood. When we said that we did, he told us that Hiba had designed it, and she smiled politely but didn't say anything. Not long after sitting down I brought up the camera we had lost, but Ateef made a face of subtle disdain and didn't reply. I took the hint and dropped it, and we returned to our polite, halting conversation.

Ateef told us that he and Nasif were from North Sudan, and that Ateef's family were from Egypt before that. He said he was a "fair-skinned" Arab from the North, and that because his people came from the desert, where people had no choice but to rely on each other, they had a culture of hospitality that was not present in the South. They said nothing of Ismail and his brown-black skin. After we had finished our drinks, Ateef suggested we go to the airport to see if we could get the camera.

As we were leaving, Ismail asked if I'd like to travel with him, so the two of us followed the plush 4x4 in Ismail's Škoda, which had leather seats and smelled like essential oils and cigarettes.

The airport car park was empty. In awkward silence, Ismail and I watched George, Ateef and Nasif walk across the car park into the airport. Once they were out of view, I offered Ismail a cigarette and we got out of the car to smoke. From where we were standing, I could see Hiba still sitting in the 4x4, but she didn't look at us and Ismail didn't invite her over, so I said nothing. She was looking at her mobile phone.

"We've come to this airport a lot, for business reasons," said Ismail.

"Yeah?"

"We need to collect our goods, you know, before the taxman can collect our goods. Just recently we imported some electrical items, and they want to tax them one hundred percent of their value, so we made a deal with the boss there. He says to his colleagues, 'OK to tax these, we need to go to Asalaya, to a special tax office for goods like these.' So we all leave the airport with the goods together and of course the boss gets some money too."

"Why is the tax office in Asalaya and not Khartoum, the capital?"

"What? Oh," said Ismail, before letting out a burst of laughter and screwing up his eyes, his legs buckling under his huge frame. "Jay, nothing is in Asalaya. It's the desert. You can't get an ice cream in Asalaya."

Ismail called corruption the "African way."

We smoked cigarettes and I reenacted a Michael McIntyre skit about British people at airports, about how you can always spot the British at airports because we follow the little zigzagging rope alleyways to the dot, even if there's not another single person in sight. Ismail laughed, but he was too polite to join in on the joke; because really the joke was that the British are dorks. While we were talking, a young man with pinprick pupils and scruffy clothes approached and spoke to us in perfect English. He asked me where I was from and how long I was in Khartoum, and when I started to tell him that I'd be there for something like a week, Ismail cut in, "He's here two days," he said. "He leaves tomorrow." And I remembered the first chapter of my travel guide for Sudan that was dedicated to kidnapping and felt like a fool.

For a while the young man was left rubbing his scraggly beard in silence, ignored by us, before he eventually walked away. Around then, Ismail got a phone call, and after a quick conversation in Arabic he turned to me and said he needed to see some friends.

We climbed back into Ismail's Škoda, which he called his "German car," and we drove to another part of Khartoum that was a labyrinth of polluted, cramped alleyways with groups of young men sitting and smoking hookahs on stairs outside of buildings. I had never been anywhere like it. The whole place felt sketchy. I started thinking about the modern slavery I'd read about, which was supposed to be a huge issue in Sudan, and that really I had no idea who Ismail was, and when a group of young men walked up to the car looking straight at me, I was on the verge of losing all composure, jumping out the door and running away. I relaxed slightly when I noticed how Ismail's face lit up when they reached us. They climbed into the Škoda behind me and slapped Ismail's shoulder and shook his hand, and then slapped my shoulder and shook my hand too, saying, "Assalamu alaikum" just like my friends in England might say,

"You alright mate?" And I looked at the paper carrier bags they were holding, saw that they were filled with bottles of booze, and felt alright again.

We listened to some Nigerian pop music as we drove the three men to a party, then went back to see George and the others, who had managed to get our camera and hard drives back. Then Ismail took us back to our hotel.

Nasif and Ismail took us out the next evening for some food and then to one of the city's outdoor cafes. As we sat by the Nile drinking our coffee, Ismail showed us where they were building a new mosque near the riverside, which would be the largest in that region of the city. You could see the oval scaffolding lit up by the moon reflecting off the river.

"I don't know," Ismail said, shrugging. "You understand? I'm a Muslim, I'm OK with mosques, but we already have so many. I would rather see them build hospitals. Or schools."

Ismail was from further south in Sudan, where his mother made and sold moonshine for a living. He had moved to Khartoum for work and said that ninety percent of men in Sudan were drinkers. Nasif asked us if we drank, and we said we did and that really it was unusual for people to not drink in England, unless they were Muslim. When we asked Nasif if he drank, he laughed and said no, and I thought he looked coy, an expression that sat strangely on his grey-bearded face.

Over the next couple of days we became increasingly uncomfortable in Khartoum. We liked and trusted Ismail, but Ateef and Nasif kept popping up everywhere and "helping" us, talking to the locals on our behalf or ordering taxis for where we wanted to go. They did it whether we wanted their help or not. They would appear together, and then normally Ateef would leave, with Nasif left running the show, organising things and making plans for us. We were unsure about Nasif's character. To us he was unfailingly polite, but on a few occasions when beggars approached us he acted with unbridled hostility, near violence. George and I couldn't find it in us to like him after that. We didn't want Ateef's help. Everyone we met in the city was so helpful that we didn't need any more help.

We were getting concerned that Ateef was going to hit us with a bill for everything they'd done for us before we left. We had been given the contact details of the company in Port Sudan, so the day after our visas had been verified we woke up early to get ourselves a bus ticket out to the coast, which was five hundred miles away. While we were looking for a tuk-tuk driver to take us to the bus station, Nasif and Ismail turned up out of nowhere; when we told them what we were doing, Nasif was determined to give us a lift. We talked our way out of it by saying that we wanted to ride a tuk-tuk because they look fun, and after he had mulled it over Nasif shrugged and called a tuk-tuk driver over, a young man with a strong jaw and skin that was a deep brown, almost black. Nasif put one foot on the driver's tuk-tuk while he spoke to him in Arabic. He spoke for a long time. The younger man didn't look up once but kept his eyes on the ground. When Nasif had finished speaking he pushed the driver in the arm, making the tuk-tuk rock from side to side, and then came over to us.

"I've told him to take you safely to the bus stop," Nasif told us. "From there he will buy you a ticket at the station and then he will take you back here. He will not charge you more than three hundred pounds. Do not pay him more than three hundred pounds." We thanked Nasif and left his company forever.

On the tuk-tuk ride we ripped through the city, between moving vehicles, passing through spaces two millimetres wider than the tuk-tuk at twenty-five miles an hour. George had been on one before and kept himself steady by holding onto the roof, deep in thought. I was rattled around like a rag doll.

"Did you notice how the driver wouldn't even look at him?" George asked me, and I said that I did, and that I thought he was scared. I thought the young driver still looked unsettled as he drove us to the bus stop.

———

The bus to Port Sudan was perfumed and had colourful, patterned fabrics hanging over each seat. The driver drove at full speed the entire way. Twice during the journey, we were each handed a syrupy fruit drink in a small plastic bottle and an individually packaged spiced sponge cake. We stopped periodically along the way for people to go to the toilet, even though it is impossible to find a place to hide in order to take a piss in the desert. The first time we stopped, I walked around until I found a ditch, and knelt down to try and hide myself from view but regretted it when I realised midstream that a few hundred other people had picked the same spot before me.

After each stop we'd all pile into the coach again, which had a television screen in the middle of the ceiling. I couldn't see the TV screen, but I could hear it being broadcast loudly around the bus on little speakers situated every couple of seats. Initially, whatever was on the television was unremarkable; a chat show broken up by cheesy adverts. But in the middle of the broadcast there was a section with a man praying live. I could tell by the way he said 'Allah' a lot and by the tone of his voice. It lasted for maybe ten minutes, with the man getting more and more frantic until he was crying while still praying, repeating the same phrase about God over and over, his voice distorted through his sobbing. No one on the bus seemed to pay it much attention.

My guidebook said there was a youth hostel on the beach at Port Sudan, so when we disembarked, we took a taxi there, agreeing on the price with the driver first, bartering by drawing numbers in the sand. He drove us to the waterfront, and we piled out and walked up to a long building lining the beach like an army barracks. Inside we found a few young men washing their clothes by hand. They greeted us, and when we showed them the map in my guidebook, they said that we were in the right place.

We looked around; the toilets were filthy, and not all of the young men staying there had beds. We smoked cigarettes with some of the guys who were apparently there on a school trip, bar one stoned guy who was an artist who had moved to Port Sudan to try to make some money. He showed us his paintings that he kept stacked up against the breeze-block wall: portraits of women and children painted in blocks of bold colour. From the hostel you could look across the beach, which was empty save for a few palm trees, and the water was the colour of blue-green agate.

We called Muhammad, who was the importer running the show portside and would be getting George's truck through customs. Muhammad seemed concerned when we told him where we were staying. He was on the phone to George, but I could hear him speaking. "No, don't stay there, it's not a good place," he said. "My son will come to you, and he can find you somewhere better."

We waited by the roadside a while, looking out at the sea and smoking more cigarettes. After around half an hour, a modern pickup truck arrived, and a young, slender man climbed out. He was maybe six foot tall, wearing jeans and a T-shirt, and had long eyelashes. He introduced himself as Mustafa and shook our hands with relaxed self-confidence, speaking English with an African accent, but in it you could hear the flattened cadence of a person who had watched a lot of American TV. And when we shook hands, we did not slap each other on the shoulder first.

We spent the first day exploring the town. Port Sudan is a very different city to Khartoum. You are never far from the sea, and when the wind comes in, passing over the water, it cools everything by ten degrees. Unlike Khartoum, Port Sudan had been planned before being constructed, and the city was punctuated by huge regal buildings, entirely white, with golden statues on their roofs. Curious, we picked one and ventured inside. Upon entering we were greeted by a smartly dressed man who said it was a hotel. In the lobby there were fountains that spanned the whole wall. We found a seat, drank a coffee and used the free Wi-Fi before leaving and walking along the waterfront that was lined with small businesses, like any coastal European town. Except that a lot of these businesses were small areas of outdoor seating in which women served coffee and teas in little glass cups from their repurposed cupboards, like in Khartoum. And the drinks they served were better than anything I'd had in Paris.

The hotel we stayed in was not one of the white palaces, but a five-storey brown square that was half ornate wood and half semi-decorated East African utilitarianism. Our room had a balcony, and from it we could stand and smoke while watching the busy street below, where men selling tobacco and roasted seeds walked up and down the road making clicking noises with handmade rattles to mark their presence.

On our second day in the city, Muhammad's son, Mustafa, picked us up from the hotel to take us into the mountains. He wanted us to meet his friends. He told us that if we wanted to get there on time we would have to drive at night, even though driving at night was dangerous, as cars often didn't have working lights, and you could end up hitting another vehicle without knowing it existed until it was killing you. As we travelled, Mustafa told us about his life. He told us that he had been to university in Malaysia, as had a lot of his friends. They'd all studied business and now worked in their family businesses. George tried to film the journey on his GoPro camera but was having trouble undoing the case, which had dust clogged in the latch. Mustafa said he'd had the same problem.

"Have you ever been diving with it?" he asked George.

"A few times, but I don't have the chest mount, so it's not easy to hold while I'm diving."

"Which scuba course did you do? Did you do PADI?"

"Yeah, but it wasn't the best. Do you know what we call PADI on the ship? Pay And Dive Immediately. I've heard that SSI is actually better."

"What's the deepest you've gone?"

"Around forty metres."

"That's advanced. I've never been deeper than eighteen metres. What about you, Jay? Have you ever been diving?"

"No."

"And what about this truck you're bringing in? Is it your truck, George?"

"Yep."

"What kind of truck is it? A Toyota?" asked Mustafa.

"Yeah, a Hilux," said George.

"The best. Did you make any changes to it?"

"A few bits. I put a bigger fuel tank in it and changed the suspension."

After driving for an hour, we turned off the main road and drove up a steep path, upwards into the mountains. The path was thin and wound like a corkscrew, and we followed it for maybe ten minutes, the truck rocking left to right on the uneven terrain. Eventually, the ground levelled, and we could see the hotel in front of us. Behind it the mountains were triangles of solid black against the moonlit sky.

We parked up in the hotel car park and got out. Mustafa went to his truck and pulled a ball of hash the size of my fist from under the wheel arch, and then we walked down to the hotel where his two friends were waiting on the patio, one tall and slim and one shorter and stocky. We shook their hands in the Western way, without the hand slap on the shoulder. They were called Raheem and Aziz. Aziz had a glass of straight whisky next to him with a huge chunk of ice in it. Raheem stood, slightly stooped but still a few inches taller than me, drinking orange juice from a tall glass with a moulded, patterned base.

Mustafa invited us to sit, and Aziz apologised and said he was out of whisky. Raheem, who had remained standing, laughed and said we could have some of his orange juice, but was afraid to tell us that there was no whisky in it.

"Where do you get your alcohol from?" I asked.

"You have to have, like, a dealer, I suppose," explained Mustafa.

"Do you drink, Raheem?" I asked.

"No, I don't drink or smoke cannabis."

"Do you smoke cigarettes?"

"Yes, I do sometimes."

"Do you want one?"

George shared round the cigarettes he had bought in the airport and we all smoked.

"We were told it was forty lashes for drinking here," said George.

"Yeah, but a lot of people drink; you just can't be seen to be drunk," said Mustafa.

"It's more like if you drink and become a nuisance you may get the lashes," said Aziz. "Otherwise, no one should care."

"I actually got them once," said Mustafa. "They weren't that bad. They didn't do it too hard. It was more that I found it embarrassing, you know?"

"What about smoking weed? Is that OK as long as you don't cause a nuisance?" I asked Mustafa.

"No, man. Drugs are illegal here."

We stayed the next two weeks in Port Sudan, spending each evening with our new friends. In the daytime, while Aziz and Raheem and Mustafa worked, George and I would hang out in the hotel or walk around the town or try to get updates on our truck, which arrived into the port a few days after us but continuously failed to make it through customs. The port officials kept telling us that it would be processed tomorrow, inshallah. When the time zones matched up and I could get a good enough Internet connection, I'd call Rishni and we'd talk, but opportunities were fleeting.

Mustafa told us about the different ethnic groups in that part of Sudan. He pointed to one of the men selling cigarettes and seeds and said that he was Beja, who were an indigenous people of Eastern Africa, famous for breeding the best camels. Mustafa said you could tell that the cigarette seller was Beja by the little waistcoat he wore over his thobe—the flowing white robe worn by most Sudanese men. Mustafa told us there were literally hundreds of languages in the country, and a few times he spoke to street vendors in languages I knew were not Arabic, even though Arabic was Mustafa's mother tongue. He said it was a good thing to talk to people in their own language if you could.

Mustafa, Raheem and Aziz all disliked their government intensely. They said that as Omar al-Bashir had made his place as leader through violence, his entire time in office had therefore been based on violence, and that he spent their country's resources killing others because of old family feuds that should have been forgotten a hundred years ago.

"Is this what most people think about him here?" I asked.

"Yes, of course," said Aziz. "Most people don't want endless war. Not just in Sudan, but in any country. Although I'm sure you read all sorts of stories about Sudan and Africa when you are at home, and it must seem like a savage place." Aziz, who was the most political out of the three, and a businessman to the core, was generous-hearted but bull-headed. When he'd made up his mind, it was his way or no way. "But still, we have our differences," he said. "Like in England, people have babies without being married?"

"Some do, yes."

"That's very disgusting in Sudan. And I think that at one time it was disgusting in England too. But now you've lost that part of your culture."

"It used to be very unacceptable," I said. "They used to send women to institutions if they got pregnant without being married, but now generally I don't think anyone would have an issue with it."

"And you know why this is? Why you lost your culture?" asked Aziz. "Because you lost your religion. If you had kept Christianity, you would have retained your culture; but now you are losing it to America."

Aziz's beliefs were a mixture of principled sensitivity and old-world conservatism. I found a lot of his views contradictory when considered from my own understanding of left and right-wing politics. Despite the drinking of straight whisky and pot smoking, Aziz had clear and strong beliefs about the loss of morality in the West, which he felt we should be concerned about; but then he would find it hard to accept some of the more unforgiving elements of our society. When I told him a criminal record could end my career as a nurse, he was obviously troubled.

"That's not very good, because I believe in the second chance," he said.

Mustafa was a party boy. He told us that he had started praying recently, but primarily he seemed to be concerned with having a good time. Raheem was the most religious and was kind-hearted to a fault. He liked playing chess and watching sensationalist Nigerian soap operas. The three of them paid for everything the entire time we were there. They wouldn't let us put our hands in our pockets once.

Towards the end of our time in Port Sudan, we spent a day with Aziz while he worked. His office was a bare metal hut built from scaffolding and corrugated iron. It was situated on the stretch of road on the outskirts of Port Sudan that was home to all the automotive businesses. He had one employee, who brought us little cups of coffee from a street-seller down the road, and we drank it as Aziz worked, which mainly seemed to involve the sale of car parts.

Mechanics came to him and described what they needed, and he handed the parts over to them. Each business transaction was preceded by a warm greeting and the traditional Sudanese handshake. On a few occasions, Aziz didn't have what the men needed, and he spent some time on his phone speaking in Arabic, securing the parts from elsewhere. I noticed that Aziz was paid the money upfront only half of the time. I asked him how he'd know if they'd pay him back, and he said he didn't worry about it.

"They'll pay me," he said.

Later in the day, Raheem came and sat with us while Aziz concluded his business. Across the road more Sudanese businessmen walked from shop to shop, talking to each mechanic. Two of them had huge, bushy beards that were combed straight downwards.

"Look at these guys," said Aziz. "They look like they want to be in Daesh."

"Do you two know Daesh?" asked Raheem.

"They'll call it ISIS," said Aziz.

"Those two men are in ISIS?" asked George.

"No, but they look like they want to be," said Aziz. "They should cut their beards; it's not a good look."

It took two weeks for our truck to get through customs. When it was finally done, we found that its entire contents were turned upside down, and the booze George had left in it by mistake was missing. We spent the morning packing up, and then went for one last coffee with our new friends, giving as a gift a framed photo we had taken of us all in the mountains when we had first met. As we said goodbye, I felt genuine regret, and George and

I both agreed we would return to Port Sudan.

Then we climbed into the truck and started moving, honking our horn while Aziz, Raheem and Mustafa, and a bunch of people in the street who we'd never even met, all waved us goodbye. And then onto the road, which in that part of Sudan is always long and straight, and cuts through the desert like a laser.

4

Never Getting Dry

The Walk to Spain—Two

The morning the ferry arrived in France I woke up late. I'd been up until the early morning drinking in the ferry bar and was woken by an announcement over the Tannoy saying it was time to disembark. I threw my stuff together and walked into the French morning hungover and disorientated.

Roscoff was a handsome coastal town built in grey-green stone, with a row of shops near the water's edge, but the morning was grey, cold and ruthless. I found a bakery with two kindly, plump women my mother's age working behind the counter. In my terrible French I asked for two croissants to compensate for the breakfast I had missed on the ferry. I then found a public toilet on the harbour and tried to fill the two two-litre water bottles I was carrying in the sides of my backpack. The sink was so small that I had to crush the bottles to get them under the tap. When I pulled them out, I crushed the bottles again and some of the water was pushed back out, spraying onto the floor, meaning that I only had a few litres to walk with.

Once I felt that my supplies were in order, I guided myself out of Roscoff with a road map I'd bought in England. I had chosen the map because it listed cycle paths and country roads as well as the larger motorways. My plan was to get to the Nantes–Brest canal by taking these smaller roads and cycle paths, and then to walk the three hundred kilometres to Nantes using the canal. Once in Nantes I would be able to get my bearings again and buy more maps. As I circled the town looking for the right road, I came across drawings of shells on lampposts that I recognised as the way-markers for the Camino de Santiago, the trail that would have guided me all the way to Cape Finisterre had I followed it. There was a moment of deliberation where I considered following the route marked by the shells, but I didn't want to give up on my plan before I'd even started. I found the road that I thought should take me to Plouénan, the next town that I hoped would get me one step closer to Spain.

I left Roscoff along an empty country road, through scraggly farmland made barren by the winter. By midday I had reached Plouénan and felt elated, but the triumph of reaching my first milestone in France was dashed when I realised that my map only provided thorough details of the roads that connected each town and contained almost no details of the roads in the towns themselves. Unable to find my way out of Plouénan, I had to ask for directions from an elderly farmer who couldn't understand my French and ended up sending me five miles back towards England; I worked out that I'd gone wrong when my compass had been pointing north for an hour straight. I turned around and found the right path without anyone's help, but for the rest of the day I despised every French man, woman and child on the planet. Desperation begets prejudice.

And that night when I settled down to camp it was cold. For the first time since starting my walk, doubt had begun to creep in. I lay in my tent that I'd pitched up in another empty field and spent the hour before I slept drained of excitement by the strain of the walk, wondering what the fuck I was actually doing. The grey sky over the wet field miles from anyone I loved and the cold that ripped through my thermals any time I needed to leave my tent to take a piss—it was all so utterly uncompromising. I hadn't experienced anything like it before. As I listened to the wind and thought about it, I realised that never in my life had a set of circumstances cared so little about me; I felt an absurd wave of indignation rising within me, but I quelled it: The winter didn't care if I froze to death in my sleep, and outrage wasn't going to change that. And anyway, I wasn't turning back. The winter could come and take me, but I wasn't turning back.

The next day, I moved through more empty farmland to Guimiliau, then into a nature reserve called Parc naturel régional d'Armorique, making my way to a town called Saint-Rivoal, which sat in the middle of the reserve. As I moved from town to town, I devised a system: I used the towns as markers, knowing that I couldn't have gone too far wrong if I was able to identify the last town I had passed through. The churches in each town were reliably marked on the map, so when I got to a town I'd try and find the church before orienting my way further south using my compass and road signs. Each town was a reliable resource, and I'd make use of the buildings in each one as shelter, setting up my camping stove on the steps of the town hall or a bus stop. The townspeople who passed me—filthy, with my long black hiking coat, cooking porridge while sitting on the ground—seemed genuinely disturbed by my presence. Some looked concerned while others were openly repulsed.

I made the porridge with water and mixed strawberry-flavoured protein powder into it. I ate three bowls a day; and for the first little while I generally enjoyed it, as long as I had enough water, which I collected from streams and sterilised with chlorine tablets. When I was low on water, the porridge would always end up dry and claggy, sticking in my throat as I ate it. To supplement my diet of porridge I stocked up on sweet pastries or bread anytime I passed a bakery. Fresh fruit and vegetables were not an option, as I passed no open supermarkets or greengrocers. Along with my porridge I took a multivitamin each morning.

Far worse than the porridge was the shitting. I despised shitting outside. I could not get used to it. If possible, I would wait until I got to the nearest town and look out a public toilet, which were always ice cold and more fitting to a prison cellblock than a genteel French town. In Guimiliau, I used a public toilet that was like a dungeon. The only source of light came from a doorless opening that let in tendrils of pale sun stained white by the winter cloud cover, accompanied by ice-cold winds. Like most of the toilets in that part of France, it didn't have a sit-down facility, offering just a hole in the ground to squat over. I shat in the hole without hesitation, keeping my balance by placing as little of my fingertips as I could on the sodden floor. When I was done, I went to wash my hands but couldn't find a sink. After searching, I realised there was a tap sticking out of the stone wall, but with no basin. I washed my hands in the freezing water, which spilled onto the floor and soaked my trousers and then drained slowly into the hole on the other side of the room through which I had just shat. I have never felt such lack of reprieve as in the public toilets in Guimiliau.

After leaving Saint-Rivoal, it took nearly another day to reach the end of the nature reserve. I had been finding my way by following cycle paths until I came to Pleyben, which was home to the first big supermarket I'd encountered since leaving Plymouth. I bought a wedge of blue cheese and some fruit, and ate the cheese spread over crisp apples that I had cut into slices. It was the first fresh fruit I'd had since arriving in the country.

Once I'd eaten, I followed a small footpath south until I came across a body of water tucked into the bottom of a wooded hill. I wasn't sure if I had reached a canal or if it was just another river, so I hurried down to take a closer look, kneeling at the water's edge to find that the bank was man-made and ran as straight as a ruler. An elderly couple were walking their dog by the waterside, and I asked them if it was the canal that went to Nantes, excitement making my voice shrill. They told me that it was.

"Je vais à Nantes," I said, and pointed in the direction that I thought Nantes was in; then I said, "Je vais à Brest," and pointed in the opposite direction. The old woman said that I was right, while the old man smiled impishly.

"Nantes? Ce soir?" he said and looked at his watch. "Je ne sais pas…"

That night, I pitched up my tent by the edge of the water. When I was set up, I called home from my mobile. I hadn't had a real conversation with anyone for nearly a week. When I got through, my mum passed the phone around to my brother and my dad so that I could update them on my progress. I could tell that finding the canal meant almost as much to my family as it did to me. I gave them my location and they looked it up on the map. We plotted the previous towns I had passed through so they could see my progression.

After the call I got into my tent and took my boots and socks off. I was genuinely disturbed by the way my feet looked. Many of the blisters had filled with blood, whereas others had burst and corroded into open wounds. I felt the layer of sweat and rain on me like oil, and my boots were sodden again. When my feet got wet, they seemed to blister more. I packed each boot tightly with an old newspaper I'd picked up in Guimiliau to absorb some of the moisture before I started walking the next day.

My water bottles were empty again, so I couldn't brush my teeth. I lay in my tent running my tongue across the fur on my front teeth wondering how long it took to die of thirst, then thought of my mum and dad at home in Devon. And I missed my dog. I missed living a life in which I didn't need to worry about finding clean water or keeping my feet dry.

The path that followed the canal was lined with little tombstone-shaped signs that counted down the distance to Nantes. These new visible markers of my progress spurred me on, and I started setting myself goals: ten kilometres before my next cigarette, twenty kilometres before I could stop to eat. On my first day walking the canal I noticed raindrops making little dark circles on the water next to me, yet I remained dry. I put my hand out over the water and little spots of rain collected on my knuckles. It was raining into the canal but not onto me. I was astonished. There was no shelter above me, but I guessed the rain had to stop somewhere. I pulled my hand back and sucked the rain from my fingers, which were salty with the filth of not being washed properly for days, and then I started walking again, the rain falling next to me as a companion.

I spent a few days like this, tramping along and daydreaming while scanning the path for the little tombstones to count my progress, and then tramping some more. The canal was almost entirely deserted. If I happened to pass close to a town, I might see a lone dog walker who I would exchange a single word with in greeting, but other than that it was just me on the canal. As a result, my daydreaming was allowed to progress uninterrupted. I spent days planning how I'd spend a lottery win: elaborate trust funds that would get my friends through university without actually putting anything in their holey pockets, a lavish library requiring a ladder that you had to slide from one genre to another, and an egocentric bid to help the developing world. I also had a recurrent fantasy in which I defended my girlfriend from an attacker, breaking a beer bottle over his head before jumping into a car and speeding away with her.

No matter how deep the daydream went, my thoughts would always eventually return to friends and family. I wanted to be with them all so much that thinking of them caused me almost physical pain. Treasured memories became agony. I learnt to numb myself by redirecting my thoughts as soon as I began to think of someone I loved. If I did this quickly enough, I could avoid becoming overwhelmed. It worked best when I focused on future plans, which acted like a riptide and pulled me away from sentimentality.

Small comforts were important. I smoked cigarettes that I rolled with raw American Spirit tobacco wrapped in thin OCB papers. As I smoked, I drank instant coffee that I made by boiling stream water on my portable stove. There was no other respite physically. After a week of tramping, it had grown so cold that I was forced to wear thermals throughout the day and night, which gave me a rash around my ankles. My tent also had a bad condensation problem, and each morning water would drip onto me as I lay in my sleeping bag. I went from a damp tent into damp hiking clothes into the damp day. I hadn't had a proper shower since leaving the ferry, and the combination of the sweat and the moisture was causing skin to break down wherever it met other skin: armpits, inner thighs, between my toes. Red patches speckled with gummy, white flesh developed; blobs of globular tissue that could be scratched off with a thumbnail.

I was taking a little break, leaning against one of the canal's locks, when a cyclist stopped to see what I was doing. He was a young man with grey skin and sharp, yellow teeth. After throwing out a few words in French he began talking in fluent English.

"Are you a walker?" he asked me.

"Yep."

"Where are you walking to?"

"I'm walking to Spain."

"To Spain?" he asked, incredulous.

"Well, tonight I just want to get a few miles further south, and then I'll camp somewhere at the side of the canal. That's what I've done every night so far."

"But what about the cold?"

"What about it? It's horrible but there's nothing I can do about it."

"Tonight, they are saying that it will be minus-twelve degrees Celsius and that we can expect snow. I think you should think about finding a hotel for tonight. Camping in this weather, I don't know what will happen to you," he said and laughed.

I couldn't take my eyes off his pointed, yellow teeth.

"Yeah, well I'm prepared. I've been camping in the cold for a little while now. Is there a hotel nearby?"

"In my village there's a bar that sometimes accommodates people. They might be able to offer you a room. I can check for you?"

I thought about the spongy rash on my ankles and said OK, why not, and he told me that he would cycle to his village and ask for me, and then meet me a few kilometres down the canal at a bridge, where he would be able to let me know what they said.

The man cycled away and I started marching again. Slowly, the prospect of staying inside began to consume me. I imagined a hot shower and hot food. Food that wasn't vitamin tablets or protein powder mixed into porridge. I realised that I hadn't sat on a soft surface like a couch for nearly a week. When I was on the ferry, I read that sitting on cold surfaces could give you haemorrhoids. From then on, I'd smoked my cigarettes standing up. More than a soft surface, I wanted to be dry. Ten days of sweat and rain had left a residue that clung to my skin like paint.

But the sharp-toothed man never came. Nor did the bridge. I walked for ten miles and didn't see either. Twice I passed empty chalets that looked like they provided accommodations to tourists in the summer. When I came to the second set I peered through the window and could see electric heaters and bunk beds. The door was locked, but for a while I lingered outside, considering forcing the flimsy wooden door open, even going so far as to push on the top corner, which flexed inwards easily. But I couldn't find the will to force it open entirely. Instead, for the first time since leaving Devon, I broke my own rules and walked into the night hoping to find the sharp-toothed man and his hotel; but after hours of marching, I was forced to give up and pitch my tent under torchlight.

A busy road with articulated lorries travelling along it ran parallel to the canal where I had stopped. It was a dangerous spot, but I was so tired that I pitched up regardless. I crawled into the tent, and from my sleeping bag listened to the passing vehicles travelling along at seventy miles an hour. They made a noise like a hiss mingled with thunder. I imagined a lorry coming off the road in the ice and ploughing through the flimsy steel fence straight into me as I slept, obliterating my tent like a hammer hitting a meringue. Before I fell asleep, I vowed that soon I would find a hotel, of any kind, and that I would get that shower and wash my clothes.

By the afternoon of the next day, I did find a hotel; I just had to walk a mile or so off the canal into a town called Pontivy to get to it. I was shown the way there by an elderly couple who were out walking along the canal after their lunch. I described my trip to them as best as I could, and they wished me 'bon courage'. They led me up a small footpath into the centre of the town, where the taller buildings were decorated by hand-painted, weather-beaten advertisements, probably each forty years old.

I stopped at the first hotel I found, where a depressed-looking man with thinning black hair showed me to a rundown room with yellow wallpaper and orange bedclothes. I dropped my stuff at the foot of the bed and showered. When climbing out of the shower, I caught my reflection in the bathroom mirror and was shocked by my appearance. My ribs stuck out and my shoulders seemed to have narrowed; my new beard was patchy, and the skin on my face and hands had turned red-brown through the constant exposure to the sun and wind. I had only been walking a little over a month but looked like a survivor of a shipwreck. I texted a good friend who had done a lot of trekking to tell him about my weight loss, and he texted back saying that I probably needed to eat a lot more calories than I was, especially if I was camping in the cold.

I washed some underwear in the sink and hung them to dry over the radiators, then went downstairs and drank a few beers in the desolate bar with the depressed-looking hotelier. He told me that since the recession had hit, a lot of people in France didn't have the money to drink in bars, so we probably wouldn't have any company. After an hour or so I went upstairs to my room and watched French softcore porn being broadcast on television, smoking the Lucky Strikes I'd bought from the bar. My drying underwear made the air around me humid as the radiator cooked the moisture into the room.

I left the hotel the next day knowing I'd gone soft for having a night indoors. I hadn't been on the road an hour before I missed the warmth of the hotel and the company of the barman. The day was made worse by the fact that I had drank the water from the taps in the hotel without purifying it and it had given me the shits. This meant that I had to keep stopping to climb through the foliage growing along the footpath in order to find a place to crap. It broke my rhythm. On one occasion, when scrambling out of a bush, I came across a dead otter with its leg completely torn off. It lay desecrated amongst the frost-covered leaves like an omen. I was amazed by its size, and that something had been able to kill it. The otter's tail was pure muscle and six inches thick at the base. From my perspective of loneliness and cold, it felt like a communication of something; I had always loved otters. I shook these thoughts off and got walking again.

The cold persisted. Each day it snowed periodically in brief, hectic flurries; and the cod liver oil tablets that I was taking, in a bid to protect my joints from the strain of the walk, froze solid in my rucksack. Each morning I couldn't pack my tent away with my thick winter gloves on, as I couldn't grasp the smaller components with my fingers covered. So I had to do it barehanded, working until my hands went numb from contact with the frost that had collected on the tent's exterior overnight. When this happened, I'd have to put my gloves back on and wait until I had mobility back in my fingers. Then I'd take the gloves back off and start packing up again. After a little while they'd go back to being numb, and I'd have to put my gloves on and wait another five minutes before I could re-start the work. My water bottle was frozen each morning too, and so I started each day walking with the bottle tucked into my coat to melt the ice. When I'd stop to eat or smoke, I threw stones into the canal, trying to punch holes in the ice that covered its surface.

By the time I reached the town of Josselin, there was less cloud cover and the air had warmed slightly in the midday sunshine. I didn't want to waste more time straying from the canal, but Josselin looked so pretty, with a castle that had ornate, pointed turrets bordering the water, that I thought I'd have a look around. It felt like something from a fairy tale. I needed to find somewhere to wash my clothes anyway.

As I started up the path that ran past the castle, I passed a young man who smiled at me and gave a polite "Bonjour." I took the opportunity to ask him if there was anywhere in the town that washed clothes, but I couldn't remember the French word for laundrette, so I asked him where I could find a shower for my clothes. Looking confused, he said in French, "Yes, OK, at my house," and motioned for me to follow him. We walked back out to the outskirts of town in near silence.

I sensed that he may have gotten the wrong end of the stick halfway through the walk to his house, and when we finally reached where he lived, and he was showing me to his shower room, he looked at the bundle of clothing I had taken out of my bag and asked, "Just a shower, yes?" and I said, "Yes, just a shower," embarrassed, but took my clothes anyway because I couldn't think of a way to put them down without confusing things further.

The shower was like a baptism, even if I did have to put on my dirty clothes afterwards. When I went back downstairs, my new friend had filled the table in his kitchen diner with a meal for us both: bowls of soup, bread, cheese, fruit and a large chocolate bar resting on its opened wrapper. As we ate, I had my first-ever conversation in another language. The young man's name was Pierre, and he was a landscape gardener. As I talked, he kept saying, "Tu seul?" as I described my trip, which is French for 'By yourself?' He seemed particularly concerned when I told him that I had been walking at night. He also wanted to know where it was possible to pitch a tent on the canal without being bothered. After we had finished eating, Pierre made strong black coffee and rolled two liquorish cigarettes without filters, which we smoked outside his house in silence because I had nothing more I could say to him in French; and he, like many of the people I had met working in that sparsely populated area of France, didn't speak English and didn't waste words.

I left Pierre and followed the canal for another one hundred and fifty kilometres. I thought a lot about suicide. As I trudged along the canal, I decided that once I had finished the walk, I would never be able to consider committing suicide again. Loneliness hung around me and was infinitely worse than the blisters or the cold, and the severity of that loneliness was for me evidence of how much I loved everyone close to me. I felt that it would be impossible to kill myself with that new knowledge. The loneliness was by then a constant companion. It would swell up after spending time with other people, and my lunch with Pierre had done it that time. It would take time, but I knew I'd grow accustomed to the solitude again.

The physical difficulties persisted. The cold didn't want to shift, water remained scarce and some nights it took a long time to find a good spot for my tent. But by then I was just fine with making do with what was available. One night, towards the end of the cold snap, I had no choice but to camp on a roundabout on a road not far from the canal, as it was the only place where the ground was soft enough to get my pegs in. As I hunkered down, the lights of passing cars shone into my tent, their headlights tracing circles on the fabric as they drove around me, but I managed to sleep soundly, hugging my water bottle to my body to keep it from freezing.

———

As I neared the end of the canal, I stopped at a restaurant where I ate a three-course meal of pigs in blankets and chips, fish and potatoes, and a chocolate pudding. It was a rural pub, busy with farmworkers and one cyclist, who asked me what I was doing. When I told him, he screwed up his brow and blew a burst of air through his lips, which I took to mean that he either was impressed or thought I was absurd. Then he patted my shoulder and said in a bemused tone, "Espagne, à pied..." while walking back to his table.

Another man, who looked like an agricultural worker, was sitting at the back of the bar, drinking heavily. He kept walking past me to take a piss outside, and from the table where I was sitting, I could see his piss steaming in the cold. Later, I saw him speaking to the cyclist and looking over at me; from then on, each time he passed me he patted my shoulder and winked at me. When I went to leave, the barwoman insisted on filling my water bottle with juice and wouldn't take any money. Like everyone I'd met since I'd left my parents' house in Devon, no one in the pub asked why I was walking to Spain.

The night before I got to Nantes, I rolled into a town called Sucé-sur-Erdre. I found a supermarket where I stocked up on eggs, fruit, bread, pâté and a huge array of sweets. In the shopping queue I asked the woman in front of me if there was a hostel in the area, as I was sick of the cold. She asked me to wait while she paid and then called several friends on her mobile before saying, in pinched-off English, that she knew some hotel owners but was very sorry she couldn't find anything that I could afford, even though I hadn't mentioned anything about how much money I had. Before I had a chance to thank her and walk away, she asked me if I might like to stay at her house, with her and her husband, for the night.

"You don't mind?" I asked.

"No. We are happy to have you in our home."

"OK. Yes, thanks. Really thanks."

"My name is Patricia," she said, and we shook hands.

She let me pack up my shopping and then we walked to her 4x4. When we got to the car, she lifted my bag into the boot herself.

Patricia's husband was still working, so we went to his office so she could tell him that I was staying. As we waited outside for him, I wondered if they might be swingers. The office was an ornate, modern building made of wood and glass, surrounded by dense woodlands. When Patricia's husband finally emerged, he walked confidently over to me and shook my hand, introducing himself as Bernard.

"Are you walking the Camino de Santiago?" he asked me. I hesitated, because I both was and wasn't.

"No," said his wife, looking at me in a way that made me think she didn't want me to be. So I went with it.

"No, I've been walking the canal from Brest," I said. "And before that I walked some of the coast in England."

"OK. How old are you?"

"Twenty-one," I said. He smiled.

"And you're going to Spain?"

"Yes."

"OK," he said, seemingly satisfied, and then looked at Patricia, smiling, before saying a few words in French that were too fast to catch. He turned back to me. "See you later," he said in English, and Patricia and I got back into the car.

"He will finish his work and then come home to see us later," Patricia said. "And then we can go for dinner."

At their house, which, like Bernard's office, was also huge, wooden and modern, I was shown how to use the pressure shower and then changed into the clothes that were closest to being clean. After that, Bernard returned, and we went out to a restaurant where I ate a local pork dish and drank good local cider from a clay cup. They wouldn't let me pay for anything, and I sat there, out of place in my stinking hiking clothes, loving every minute of it. After the meal, I spent the night sleeping in a comfortable bed, and in the morning they gave me fresh coffee and croissants.

Before I left, I wrote my thanks onto a postcard I had bought in Plymouth. Patricia seemed touched when I gave it to her and attached it to their fridge. The postcard was a reprint of an old black-and-white photo that showed a man on a winged bicycle in mid-flight. It wasn't a well-constructed flying device like the ones the Wright Brothers used; it was a precarious contraption that looked like it had been built in somebody's garden shed. But the man appeared serene, sailing through the air like he was on his way to work. Bernard laughed when he saw it, then asked, "Did he live?"

5

A Night in Dinder National Park

Sudan to Kenya—Two

From Port Sudan, George and I drove in the truck back to Khartoum. We didn't want to go back, but there was only one road south from Port Sudan and that was where it went. It took us a day to reach the capital, and we stayed the night in a campsite in the city, sleeping in the tent on top of the truck before moving on the next day to Al Qadarif, which was three hundred miles southeast of Khartoum. In Al Qadarif we bought a thirty-litre bottle of water and some dried beans, and the shopkeeper, who sat outside his shop drinking tea, invited us to eat lunch with him and his father. We ate a meal of fül and bread, and then drank hibiscus tea with lots of sugar, which his father declined on account of his diabetes. The shopkeeper spoke good English, having gone to school in an age when learning English was still a high priority in Sudan; though he admitted it was not now.

"And where will you go next?" asked the shopkeeper.

"The national park, Dinder," said George.

"Wonderful."

"We want to camp there, is it allowed?"

"I don't think it's not allowed."

I was worried about lions. I asked the shopkeeper if we needed to be on our guard for them.

"No, since the war, most of the lions are gone," he said. "And the farmers took the lions' land for their own. The few that remain are very scared of you. There are some hyenas, but they are scared too."

We finished drinking our tea and I told him that it was very good, and when we went to leave he went into his shop and came out with a sack of hibiscus tea that he gave us for the road.

We travelled across an afternoon of desert before we reached Dinder National Park, which was dry and scrubby, and the earth was so cracked it looked like a jigsaw. But the presence of trees and their meagre green leaves was a welcome reprieve after our time in the desert. We parked not far up from the road and took out our collapsible tables, cooking pots and our stove that ran on petrol, then cooked some dal made from the local beans we had bought in Al Qadarif. While we were cleaning up, two men on a motorcycle stopped and greeted us, shaking both our hands, but left when they realised we didn't speak enough Arabic to hold a conversation. As they drove off, I noticed that one of the men had an AK-47 strapped to his back.

"I don't suppose you happened to see the machine gun on that man's back?" George asked me.

"Yeah, I noticed that. What are you thinking? Should we still camp here? Or do you think we should move on?"

"No, I think it's probably fine. I just wasn't expecting it. The two guys seemed alright."

"They were nice. It's going to get dark soon. So, are we

staying?"

"Let's stay. Like you said, it will be dark soon. No one will notice us then. A lot of people probably have guns here. I don't think it's unusual."

As the light began to fade, we began setting up camp.

We hadn't been at it five minutes when we noticed a pickup truck speeding towards us, kicking up dust as it scrambled across the bone dry ground. It pulled up a few metres from us, breaking suddenly and skidding a little, the tyres scratching against the gritty earth. Two men sat on the cargo bed and two were in the cab. After the truck had stopped, they all climbed out and walked over to us. The two men who had been travelling in the front were the oldest, although there was twenty years between them. The two in the back were young—teenagers, really. All of them wore the traditional white thobe, and over the top they had Victorian-style waistcoats like the Beja people in Port Sudan; but these men were shorter and stockier, and they approached without any of the preamble or ritual of a big greeting that we had grown accustomed to in the rest of Sudan. When they reached us, the oldest man shook our hands and spoke quickly in Arabic. His voice was hoarse.

The men started going through the stuff we had on the tables. They picked up the multi-burner and George made a fire noise and then I mimed cooking on top of it. They put it down and picked up the collapsible cup, which popped out into a regular cup shape as they lifted it, and they mimed drinking. We nodded and said, *"Na'am,"* which we thought meant 'Yes,' and they laughed and tossed the cup back onto the table. They were just making sense of the pressure cooker when a yell went up from over near the truck, and we all hurried over to find the source of the noise. The youngest guy was looking through our windscreen. He turned and said something to the others.

They gathered around the window talking to each other, and then the man with the hoarse voice looked over to us and mimed driving, pointing to the right of our car where the driving wheel was. Then he pointed to their own truck and to their driving seat, which was on the left.

George said, "It's an English truck, we drive on the left." They walked back to us and said, "English? English?" to us questioningly. We said, "*Na'am*, English," and then I pointed at George and myself and said, "English."

The leader with the hoarse voice looked around our camp with some reproach and mimed sleeping. We said, "*Na'am.*" He shook his head saying, "*Laa*," which means 'No,' and then some words we didn't understand. Then he mimed something prowling, which we thought could have meant either lion or hyena, and then he gestured for us to get into our truck. Without speaking the same language, we couldn't reason with him at all, so we just packed up and did as he said. We didn't have any better ideas.

The men had taken on a new efficiency, and they organised themselves without seeming to pay any attention to us. When we were ready to go, he told the rest of the guys to get into their truck, and then he climbed in with us, giving George directions while speaking loudly in Arabic and gesturing with his hands. The other truck followed us. Although I couldn't understand them, the men felt hostile to me. I got so nervous that I had that metallic taste in my mouth that you get when your heart is beating hard. Slowly, so no one would notice, I slid my hand down the side of my seat where I kept my hunting knife and held on to it.

It was dark when we pulled into their camp, which was made

up of a few squat tents with thin wooden frames covered in thick fabric. Surrounding the camp there were patches of amber light, like campfires burning in the distance, and we could hear the sound of livestock. I couldn't identify the species on noise alone. The car stopped and children ran over to us, and the men from the other truck came and gestured for us to get out, and because I couldn't climb out with an eight-inch hunting knife, I gave in and dropped it and did what George did, following the hoarse-voiced man over to the fire, where he sat us down and we exchanged names. He said his name was something like John, and when we asked him if it was really John, he nodded and put his hand to his chest, repeating "John," so we went with it.

John went away and returned with a jug that he set down on the ground and a wooden bowl that he passed to George, which looked like it was filled with milk. He motioned for George to drink, so he did, making an appreciative noise. Then he looked at me and said that it was definitely a kind of milk, but very sweet. George tried to pass the bowl back to John, who shook his head and gently pushed it back towards George, who gave in and drank a few more sips before trying to hand it back, and when John refused to take it a third time it became clear that George was supposed to drink the lot, so he started taking big gulps again, and I laughed because the bowl was huge and I could tell that drinking all of it was hard work. It ran down George's beard as he drank. And then when George had finished, John took the bowl and refilled it from the jug and passed it to me, and I knew what to do and drank it all in one go.

When we were done, I went to the truck and dug out some photographs of Devon and of my family and showed John. I said, "England," and he looked through them with respect and fascination, saying words to me in Arabic that I didn't understand. When he was finished, John handed the photos back to me with so much care and gentleness that I thought about my eight-inch hunting knife that sat in the truck and felt ashamed. After a while, John went away and came back with a young woman who had a red headdress and a nose ring. John was speaking in Arabic, and it wasn't clear if he was asking her for something or presenting her to us. After they had talked, she went away and then returned with a small kettle, a bowl of sugar and three small cups on a wooden board. Then she poured the three of us coffee and went away again. We sipped our coffee in silence for a while before George said, "Jesus, I thought we were going to get married off then." I nearly spat my coffee everywhere, because I'd been thinking the same thing, but stifled the laugh.

John wouldn't let us get into our tent that night. Instead, he took out two camp beds for us to sleep on so that we could see the sky unobstructed. He was right to make us. With no light pollution, the stars were twice the size of those you could see in England. Each constellation was punched out against the black. George pointed them out to me and said he could navigate with them if he had a sextant. I wondered if that was how John and his family navigated when they needed to move camp. I thought about how long this way of life could really last, because there must have been a time when this was how everybody lived in that country, and I worried that if we came back in a few years, we may not be able to find John's family, or any family, living like this. Their way of life could be gone, just like the park's lions.

We spent the next morning showing our hosts how to play Angry

Birds on George's iPhone, then I played some saxophone for them and let them play a few notes, which amused the children. George and I noticed that when we showed them something fun, like the games on George's phone or my sax, the older men would always have the first go, and then it would be passed around the group in descending order of age. Since the time the young woman had brought us coffee, we had no further contact with the female members of the group.

After the sax lesson, I sat down and felt my stomach begin to churn. It was the milk from the night before. I can never drink milk without it upsetting my stomach. I asked John for the mirhad, and he pointed away from the camp. George said, "I think you can just go to the toilet anywhere away from the camp; it's what they seem to be doing." I got the loo roll from the car and found a bush to hide behind.

When I was done, I tried to burn the paper because I'd been told that in the desert the paper lasts years, blowing around in the wind like the ghosts of past shits. I lit the paper where it was on the ground, and it caught the flame quickly, but so did the surrounding scrub, which was as dry as a tinderbox. Before I knew it, the fire was fanned by the wind and was tearing along the ground towards the bush I was hiding behind. I had to stamp out the flaming turd wearing only flip-flops. It was dreadful. But the fire went out. Then I walked back to the group, where George was showing our new friends a map of our journey.

6

Nantes, Clisson, Saintes

The Walk to Spain—Three

The day I got into Nantes was the first day of warm sunshine since I'd arrived on the canal. The wall lining the canal footpath was covered in little lizards that were almost invisible behind the foliage. As I walked, they scrambled away from me, making the leaves rustle. The wall must have been full of them because the rustling followed me, like it was alive and reacting to each step I took. As I drew closer to the city, I listened to the song *Nantes* by Beirut on my iPod, which I had charged while staying with Patricia and Bernard. It was perfect.

I thought about my friends back in Devon. I planned on calling a couple of them the next chance I got. I wanted to tell them I'd been thinking about them and that they were fucking good boys, even though some of them wouldn't make eye contact when they spoke to you—boys that had always given me half of everything they had, even when they didn't have much, and would have given me more if I'd asked for it. I had always wondered how some of them would cope when they couldn't look someone in the eye and shake their hand before a job interview.

Although, I was no better. I'd moved to Bristol without them and there had been such hope about everything then, because I was getting out; but I ended up in the same cycle I'd been trapped in before, only it was sped up by the pace of the city. I made a few good friends, but beyond that I'd spent two years there and had nothing concrete to show for it, other than a new hatred for the sunrise that had been conditioned into me by two hundred comedowns—mornings spent sitting outside, chain-smoking and unable to sleep, watching the sun come up. I left Bristol because I'd made a mess of it, but I would die before I moved back to Devon. Whatever came next, I was going to make sure I did it right, but I tried not to waste time thinking about it. I'd figure it out after I reached Spain.

In a phone booth on the outskirts of Nantes, I had a euphoric two-hour conversation with my parents, and when I got into the city centre, I used an Internet café to find a hostel, where I showered and washed all my clothes in an actual washing machine. I sat in the lobby in just my thermals, writing in my journal while waiting for the clothes to dry. When this was done, I spent some time on the computer in the hostel dining room looking online for walkable routes to the Spanish border. There wasn't a lot to choose from. After a while, I capitulated and decided that I would have to walk the Camino de Santiago from Nantes after all.

The Camino had routes spanning Europe, one of which started in Nantes. If I followed that route, it was guaranteed to take me to Santiago de Compostela in western Spain; once I was in Santiago it would only take a few more days to walk onwards to Cape Finisterre. I chose the Camino primarily because it would be the easiest route to navigate into Spain, with the little shells marking the entire way. Apparently they were painted on walls, lampposts, the sides of houses—anything that happened to be on the trail. I'd been told that as long as I followed the shells, I'd get there. I could also buy books, which mapped the whole route, from a bookshop in Nantes.

I spent my time in Nantes drinking in a few of the Irish bars with a straitlaced Canadian engineering student who was backpacking through France. Then I spent an evening with a young woman called Stephanie and her boyfriend David, who I'd met while walking around the city. We played card games and ate a full home-cooked meal, and after we had finished eating, Stephanie gave me the address and phone number of a married couple she knew who were living in Clisson, which would be the next town I would pass through if I stuck to the Camino. When it was time for me to leave, Stephanie drove me to my hostel. When the news came on the car radio, she went quiet, listening to it a while before sighing in genuine anguish and saying, "Syria, it's getting worse."

The day I left Nantes, I bought three guidebooks for the Camino de Santiago that would guide me the entire way to Cape Finisterre. However, the only copies I could find directed the reader largely through written descriptions of the route, composed entirely in French, with only a basic map as accompaniment. I bought them anyway, hoping that along with the little shell markers they'd be enough.

Once I had my books, I found an Internet café and had a long video conversation with Amelia, my girlfriend at the time. She was distant during the call. Communication between us had been minimal for the past month and it was beginning to drive a wedge between us. We mostly stayed in contact through text messages and a very rare phone call, but she was seemingly getting cold feet about the whole relationship. We had been planning to move in with one another when I had finished my trip, but Amelia was beginning to have second thoughts. She would have to speak to her mum about it. But we did manage to agree that she would fly out to meet me in Spain, once I had finished my walk.

I reached Clisson half a day after leaving Nantes. During our dinner a few nights before, Stephanie had said she would tell her friends when I would be arriving so that they could keep an eye out for me. Failing that, I had their telephone number.

It had been a warm day and I was daydreaming, trundling through woodland, thinking about what Amelia's mum would have to say about her daughter's potential future with me, when I saw a tall, slim man on a bicycle watching me. As I got closer, he called my name, his face like a mischievous child. I guessed he must have been Stephanie's friend. I knew they'd been keeping an eye out for me, but it seemed amazing that he had found me before I'd even entered the town. I laughed.

"That's me. How did you recognise me?" I asked.

"Your beard. The orange colour."

"Oh really? French people don't have this colour beard?"

"It is not that common in France. Germany, England, yes. Not in France."

He put out his hand and I shook it.

"My name is Nicolas."

We walked together, Nicolas still on his bicycle, his front wheel shaking as he tried to keep his balance travelling along-side me at a walker's pace. He told me I was welcome to stay with him and his wife that night. He said that his wife Marie spoke better English than he did, so she could also show me around the town. Together we walked to their flat, first through woodlands, along a riverbank populated by willow trees with branches hanging so low they touched the water, then through the town. Nicolas told me the town had been destroyed over two hundred years ago and then rebuilt by an artist to look like a town in Tuscany. It looked almost medieval to me: A hive of bridges, alleyways and stone walls, growing outwards in layers from an ancient-looking castle. The newer-looking buildings were built from stone the colour of sand and capped with the red tiles you see in northern Italy.

We passed through the town to their flat, which was in an old building. The flat was painted white inside and decorated with sparse, Scandinavian furniture and a single potted plant. I spent the evening with them. Marie was straight-faced, almost stern, but at the same time maternal and affectionate. She went around organising my bedding and making any food I might like, and offered me a hot shower. We ate together after praying, then Nicolas went out for a few hours to see the local priest. After he left, Marie asked me to select a film from their collection and I picked one called *Bienvenue chez les Ch'tis*, a silly comedy about a postal worker who has to move from the south of France to the north, where the locals drink cider all day and can't speak properly. We watched it at her computer desk, which was the only DVD player they had in their flat.

I left the next day, shaking them both by the hand after noting their phone number down in my notebook at Marie's request, in case I needed anything. She was insistent about that. "Even just to talk," she said. And then I was heading south again, through farmland, then a nature reserve and then more farmland that, as I moved further south, became home to grape vines. As the cold lessened, the rain came, and I tramped for hours with my head bowed and my hood pulled forward to shield my face from the wet and the wind. I passed through Montaigu, La Châtaigneraie aux Coteaux and then moved on to Saint-Hilaire.

I passed through a lot of small villages. Almost all of them held at least a patisserie, a boulangerie and a café or bar. They were old towns built from local stone. If I was lucky enough to be passing through one when the rain had eased, I'd look around and find that they were always good-looking places, although every one of them had been cut in half by modern roads with enormous articulated lorries travelling on them. When a lorry passed, it always felt like it was too big for the road; the huge vehicles dwarfed the buildings and looked top-heavy, as if they might topple onto you when walking down the high street.

———

Seven days after leaving Nantes I was closing in on Saintes, which marked the halfway point between Nantes and Bordeaux. I woke and dressed in my tent, wrapping both my feet in torn-up pieces of waterproofing from my rucksack that I held in place with a generous amount of duct tape. I'd taken to doing this when the rain started, as I'd worn a hole in both of my boots and my socks absorbed water at any given opportunity. Damp grass was particularly bad, which was unfortunate, as at that time I seemed to spend most of each day trekking through fields.

After I was done wrapping my feet, I put my boots on and went to shit. I was in a farmer's field and, as I squatted in the cold, I heard the sound of a tractor approaching. In cold panic, I strained to finish the turd as quickly as I could and was still pulling my trousers up when the farmer passed by on his tractor.

He took one bemused look at me, cowering and semi-naked, and then turned back to the young boy sitting in the seat next to him, gesturing out at the field in front of them and talking. The boy was looking out to where the older man was pointing and nodded as he spoke. I watched them sail through a gap in a fence at the end of the field and out of view.

I packed up and started walking. I kept on my guard, as I had been having a lot of issues with the local dogs. As I got deeper into the French countryside, and the distances between the farmhouses grew, I began to meet more and more aggressive dogs that were seemingly given free range. A few days out of Nantes, I had been walking across a field when I saw two Dobermanns running at me. There was no fence between me and them, and I could tell by the way they ran that they wanted to kill me. They came at me with no hesitation, side by side like hunting wolves. I was about to start running when they both came to a jarring halt. When I looked more closely, I saw they had thick black collars around their necks, and I supposed they were the kind that gave electric shocks when the dogs wearing them moved out of an invisible perimeter. The two Dobermanns looked like they wanted nothing more than to reach me. They were pacing in a circle, but they never took their attention from me. They kept looking over at me while they howled and barked. I only happened to be where I was in the field by chance. I could have easily wandered to where the two dogs stood. From then on, I made sure the cosh my dad had given me was always to hand.

Not long after the old man in the tractor had passed me, I met my first dog of the day. It was a huge Golden Retriever that wouldn't let me within two hundred feet of its house, which happened to be sitting directly next to the footpath. The dog was waist-high with a sandy coat, and a real bastard. It made itself rigid, hairs standing up straight on its back, growling and barking madly at me anytime I tried to move along the path that ran past the house. I took out my piece of heavy-insulated cable and loosened my backpack, shifting it onto one shoulder, hoping that if the dog actually came at me, I might be able to throw the bag as a distraction and maybe get a lucky strike in. I knew I couldn't outrun it.

I walked sideways into the field that ran beside the house, always facing the animal, then started moving backwards, away from the house, never dropping my stare. I kept going until the house and the dog were in the distance. Once I was sure that it couldn't see me, I made my way forward again, travelling parallel to the original path for about a mile before making my way back to the safety of the little painted shells, following the Camino again.

I'd been back on the trail for about half an hour when a car reversed out of a driveway just ahead of me. As it reached the road it swerved to the side and slid into the ditch running alongside the path. The car revved its engine, the high pitch tearing through the quiet of the countryside, but the car didn't budge. I walked over to the old man who was driving and greeted him with a nod. I mimed to him that I'd push from the front while he reversed. I put my hands on the bonnet and pushed while he revved the engine again. The sound of the wheels spinning on the ground was like the tearing of a ship's sail, and a jet of mud sprayed out onto the road behind us; but the car didn't budge. We went at it again, but this time the car sank three inches into the mud without getting any closer to the road, so we both stopped. I dropped my hands to communicate defeat. A young woman stormed out of the house and berated the old man before jumping into her own car and speeding away along the country road.

The old man got out of the car, and we spoke a little. I tried telling him about the crazy dog, but he either didn't understand or didn't think it was anything worth discussing, and instead just gently nodded without speaking. I told him that I had to get going, as the days were still short, and he leant over and wrote the word 'Go' slowly and deliberately in the dust on the bonnet of his car, so I started up the road. Not long after, I met the woman who had shouted at the man earlier. She was being followed by a large, white van. She stopped the car and said, "Merci," and I tried to ask her about the dog, but she just laughed and said, "Oui," and then started driving again.

As I continued on my way, I realised that I felt comfortable. I had a growing certainty that the clinging moisture, the solitude, the rain and the cold, and the dogs—they were background music for something bigger. For the first time since I had left my parents' house a month and a half ago, I was able to look back on my life prior to the walk without any yearning for it. I started thinking about the day I had spent cycling along a canal outside Bristol with my friend Ted. We had made the trip when the weather had been sunny and gentle, and the day had served as a building block for an important friendship. I was able to have these memories without them making me feel lonely, and I found that I could enjoy them alone, like the pause after taking a mouthful of good food.

I pulled my hood up and leant forward into the rain, keeping one eye on the opened guidebook that hung around my neck in the plastic map holder and the other on my surroundings, scanning lazily for the tiny shells.

The next day, I found that I couldn't bring myself to eat porridge again. I just couldn't face it anymore. I finished the chocolate and the banana I had saved from the last time I had passed a supermarket and spent the morning smoking cigarettes when I was hungry, hoping to buy some food from the next bar or café that I passed. By around one o'clock, I had found my way to a small village called Le Douhet, which was just a few houses, a church and a bar. I made my way to the bar to see if I could order something to eat.

Inside there were three men in suits talking to the barman. The one doing most of the talking was standing in the middle and had black hair that had been moulded into a shiny helmet with hairspray. The rest of the room was speckled with people sitting at tables drinking coffee or small glasses of beer. The three men in suits were pointing to a poster with a picture of the man with the shiny hair on it, along with some bullet points written in French. The barman was saying, "D'accord, d'accord," rhythmically as they spoke to him, then he apologised, turned to me and asked what I wanted. I said, "Fais-tu de la nourriture?" and he apologised and said no, they did not do food. Out of ideas, I ordered a glass of beer and stood at the bar drinking it. The men started talking again, and the barman returned to saying, "D'accord, d'accord."

I drank half of the glass and then tried to head to the toilet. As I went to move, I felt a wave of nausea come over me and I truly thought I was going to vomit. I began to lose my balance and, to no one in particular, said, "Je ne pas bien. Je ne pas bien," and then collapsed.

When I came round, I was sitting in a chair that hadn't been behind me when I was conscious. I think a woman who had been sitting at one of the tables had put it there; she was still standing behind me, holding onto it. The barman handed me a glass of water that was sweet, like he'd mixed sugar into it. The other customers talked to each other in French and then left. I finished the first glass and the barman gave me another. I drank that too, and then sat with my head in my hands until the nausea left.

Behind me, I heard a door being pushed open and the sound of footsteps as the customers who had left reentered the bar. They'd gone home to get some food for me and handed me fruit, a baguette and some cheese. The barman went to see what he could find too and came back with some biscuits.

"How about a little red wine?" he asked in halting English.

"Non merci."

I stayed sitting for a while, eating some of the biscuits, and the three men in suits said goodbye to us all and walked out, leaving a poster of the man with the black, shiny hair on the bar. The barman picked it up, said something about politicians that I couldn't grasp and tossed it under the bar without looking at it. When I was feeling steady, I stood up and went to the barman, shook his hand and said goodbye. The woman who had saved me with the chair helped carry my bag to a patch of grass outside the town hall, where she left me to pitch my tent. Before she left, she gave my shoulder a squeeze.

That night, I went through my bag and put all that I thought I didn't need in a pile, which consisted of a few books I hadn't touched since setting off and the small portable chessboard my dad had given me. I also poured out most of the oats and all of the protein powder. There was no point keeping food I wasn't going to eat. From there on I would keep a little bag of porridge for emergencies, but I would make eating regular meals I enjoyed a priority, even if that meant leaving the path to Spain to find some food.

I found out later that when you don't eat enough, it's your liver that takes on the role of kicking out glucose into your bloodstream. When I'd started drinking on an empty stomach in the bar, my liver had probably taken on the role of breaking down the alcohol in my body, which meant it was too busy to kick out the glucose. This made my blood sugar drop. That's what had caused me to pass out.

I set off early the next morning after giving the chessboard to the maintenance man at the town hall. The rest of the pile of unneeded stuff went into the bin. I walked quickly and made it to Saintes by lunchtime. When I got there, I used my guidebook to find the abbey that housed pilgrims, where an old lady sold me a pilgrim's passport, laboriously taking out a metal money container, cashing the notes I had given her and then stamping the passport for me. When she was done, she took me up to my tiny room on the upper level of the monastery. The room was cramped, with wooden bunk beds crowding each of the four walls, but it was also astonishing. Each wall was constructed out of thousand-year-old stone—sandy-coloured bricks, each one a foot long, some with religious iconography carved into them. The little window was a slit that overlooked the abbey's grounds.

I looked at the other beds. There was no sign of other pilgrims. I had met a walker outside Nantes who had told me that very few walked across France, particularly in winter, but that I could expect to have a lot more company when I got to the Spanish border, especially as it would be spring by the time I arrived. Apparently, the numbers could be almost overwhelming on the Spanish section of the route, with so many pilgrims on the trail; it could feel more like a travelling theme park than a hiker's route.

After nearly two months alone, I had started to verbalise some of my thoughts. When making a decision, I'd ask myself questions under my breath. Sometimes I'd catch myself subconsciously naming the things I could see around me. When I realised I was doing it, I often couldn't work out how long I'd been speaking for. It was unnerving. I was worried that with too much time alone, I might be changed forever. The prospect of encountering hordes of people at the border onwards sounded just fine to me.

The two holes in the soles of my boots had worn through to the size of my fist and needed replacing. After I had dropped my bag off, I went to find the woman who had taken my money for the room. She was sitting at a table downstairs. After a confused conversation, she told me of a sports shop on the outskirts of town that she thought sold shoes.

It took me around an hour to get to the shop, which was laid out like a warehouse, with a high ceiling; the goods stacked on metal shelves served to divide the room into separate aisles. Speakers in each corner played the worst music in the world: pop singles from boy bands and contestants on The X Factor. Normally, I would have hated the place, but after three months being outside in the wind all day, the stillness and warmth of the shop was sublime. It felt good just to stand still, like I was taking a bath in warm water. You don't realise it, but modern human existence has become one of sensory deprivation. Most people spend most of their time indoors. Their houses are like cocoons. But when you live outside, you are exposed to the wind, and the sound of the wind, and you are also surrounded by other noises, like birds and bugs; you are hit by every change in temperature and the sunlight that shines straight into your eyes half the day. And if you don't like it, there's not a lot you can do about it. After three months on the road, the shop felt like a womb.

What modern life does offer is endless entertainment; stimulation of a different kind. Not like what's offered by the natural world, which slaps you around and dries out your eyes, but endless variations of human interaction that latch onto a different part of your brain. For the average person, music is now everywhere. It's in every building and on every television. You can become picky. You like some genres and artists and dislike others.

Over the previous three months, I had been unable to pick and choose these things. I would save my iPod for moments of extreme low morale, meaning I only listened to it for a few hours a week; I knew the music on it inside-out anyway. On the rare occasion I came across a television, I would find myself unable to stop watching it, fascinated, regardless of what was on. And I started to like any music I came into contact with. As I walked around the shop in Saintes, I began to move my body to the music. The employees looked at me like I was insane.

The lady at the till told me that all the shoes they had were out on the shelves, which meant there were only two pairs that fit me. One cost around eighty euros; the other nearly two hundred. The more expensive pair fit me very well. I'd never worn a pair of shoes like them; it was like they were made for my feet. The other pair fit fine. I walked around in them both and decided that the cheaper pair were probably good enough. I took them to the till, but when the cashier reached out to take them, I apologised, picked them up and walked back to the rack, where I swapped them for the expensive ones.

That night, I left my room in the abbey and bought a few cans of beer, drinking them while walking around the town. It was only a small town, but it was home to Roman architecture and lit by ornate lampposts. Their amber light bounced off the pale stone like moonlight on water. There was a warm breeze. It felt otherworldly, like I was walking in the reflection of a town. As I walked, I knew I had to keep a grip on myself: the kind of contemplation that comes with walking around alone in a beautiful town can often topple over into melancholy. Particularly at nighttime.

I walked down to the riverside and sat on a bench at the water's edge, drinking my final can of beer. A little further up the riverside, there were a few hippie squatters sitting on some public steps drinking wine from the bottle. They had dreadlocks, and their black T-shirts were cut off at the shoulders. Like a lot of the street punks I had seen in France, they had a pile of tattered books next to them. I wanted to drink with them but couldn't find it in me to approach them and introduce myself. After a while, I turned and walked back to the monastery and went to sleep.

I walked out of Saintes the next day, sad to go. I carried my tattered boots with me. Since Nantes, the trail had been marked by the occasional little pillar with a shell. Some of the pillars had piles of stones by them. A hiking local had told me that the stones were left by pilgrims as a way to mark their passing and as a sign of their self-sacrifice. A mile out of town, I came across one of the pillars with a pile of stones next to it and left my boots on top.

7

Lots of Tiny Stones

Sudan to Kenya—Three

Not long after passing over the border into Kenya, we started having electrical problems. We had Regina with us, a hitchhiker. A few miles earlier, at a police checkpoint, an officer with the largest machine gun I had ever seen had asked us to drop Regina at her home village on our way. We said no problem. She was actually the one who first realised something was wrong with the truck. Just as the sun was moving behind the horizon, she started getting anxious, saying that she could smell something burning in the front of the car. George pulled the front panel off the CD player and made me smell it.

"Does it smell like something's burning to you?" he asked me, and I had to tell him that it did.

Smoke started to rise up from behind where the panel had been removed, and we pulled over and all of us got out. It was dark by this time, even though we said we'd never drive at night. Because we didn't want to risk switching anything on until we knew what was burning, we felt that we couldn't use the light in the cab. I held a torch while George dug around in the electronics behind the CD player, cutting a foot of smouldering wiring out.

We got driving again, but slowly the lights on the dashboard and on the front of the truck dimmed and then went out completely. Regina told us that her village was close and that we could stop there for the night, so we pushed on, me leaning out the window trying to light our way with the feeble hand torch. The light didn't reach more than a half metre in front of the truck, but I hoped it would at least make us visible to any oncoming traffic. I remember thinking, *'This is how I go.'*

Regina called her brother on her mobile and he came to meet us in his car, driving ahead of us and lighting the road with his headlights so we could make it safely to the village. In the light from her brother's car, I watched the road surface turn from gravel to scrubby grass. After around twenty minutes we reached a square brick building, white-grey in the moonlight, and a young man came out and greeted us. He was wearing an army uniform and had a shaved head. Regina's brother shook our hands and left, and the soldier introduced himself as Simba. We left the truck and followed Simba to the back of what turned out to be a barracks, where four more soldiers were sitting in a circle drinking bottles of beer. We sat down with them, and they gave us each a beer. Simba was the soldier in charge and the most talkative.

"Where have you come from?" he asked.

"We were in Ethiopia this morning and crossed here into Kenya today," I said, "but we started our trip in Sudan nearly eight weeks ago. The plan is to end up in South Africa." One of the soldiers made a *'Phew'* sound.

"It is a long and tiresome journey," said Simba.

"It was today."

Once we had finished our drinks, one of the soldiers collected money from the rest of the group and then vanished into the dark, returning a bit later with a few more beers. They wouldn't take any money from us. We started talking about the safety of our trip.

"No one in England thought it was a good idea," George said, "but if you listened to the news in England, you'd never do anything. What do people think about what's on television here? Do they trust the news?"

"Here in Kenya, the news is honest," said Simba. "It's not like in some other African countries."

"I don't think we have the same trust of the media in the UK," I said. "I don't. The politicians, news organisations, big business, they all influence each other."

Simba and a few of the others nodded.

"And what about your president?" asked George. "The few Kenyans we've spoken to so far seemed to like him."

"Yes," said Simba, "he's a good man. He's actually the son of our first president."

"Is this President Kenyatta?" asked George.

"Uhuru Kenyatta," said Simba. "His father was Jomo Kenyatta."

A little while later another man joined the group. He was tall and thin with long arms, and he held a bottle of Guinness in his hand. When he spoke, he threw his long arms around. Occasionally he'd shout a few words of his sentences without warning.

"Some friends, they tell me that people in England are really racist," he said to us.

"Not everyone," I said. "I suppose it's there, but I don't think it's as bad as a lot of other countries." Then he turned away from me without saying anything and began to berate Simba and the other soldiers. He pointed at them as he talked, calling them "boy" and "soldier" rather than using their names.

"My father is the boss of these soldiers," he said, turning to us and slurring his words. "If you have any problems with them you come to me."

"OK, OK," said Simba softly. "We don't need to worry about any of that."

One by one, the soldiers made their excuses and went to bed. George and I said goodnight and went to set up our tent.

Three days later, the truck was still not fixed. The mechanic in Marsabit had been unable to give us even a diagnosis, but we had the address and phone number of a reliable mechanic in Nairobi, and George thought he could get the car started with a jump. We hoped that as long as we didn't stop at all, the engine would keep running and we'd be able to get there. If we stalled for any reason, that would probably be it.

We set off for Nairobi early with a full tank of petrol. George drove for the first half of the day and then I took over. We moved through the dry savannah quickly, passing camels loping along the side of the road; they were so large that, at first, I thought they were young giraffes. At some point after midday the road turned to gravel, and with each manoeuvre we slid a little. The tiny stones moving under the car sounded like waves breaking. On one particularly tight corner, the car slid to the side of the road as if the ground was covered in ice. We only just avoided coming off the track entirely.

"I don't know how to drive on this gravel stuff. It feels like I'm on ice," I said.

"You're going too slow," said George. "You'll get more traction if you move faster."

I increased our speed, but at the next corner I slid far enough that one of the front wheels came off the gravel completely. Somewhere during the sliding, I had jerked my foot off the clutch. The engine made a choking sound, then cut out. After sliding along without control, the new stillness of the car seemed amplified.

"Try the ignition," George said to me, and when I twisted the key, the truck fired up. "The battery must have had enough power for one more start," he said.

We moved back onto the road and carried on, making our way to the capital through the flattest and most expansive country I'd ever seen. A carpet of low, scorched shrubs and grass spread out further into the distance than it was possible to see, until eventually it was blanketed by a white mist. In that far distance there were forested mountains, green lumps partially hidden in the fog.

We didn't stop the engine once, and by four thirty that afternoon we had travelled the three hundred miles to the outskirts of Nairobi, where we hit thick traffic. For the first time, I was forced to put the truck into first gear. As we got closer to the city, the road widened into four lanes and the buildings slowly began to increase in size and number. They were square grey-and-brown constructions, many with busted business signs and adverts on the front. The buildings had an unfinished look about them, with exposed concrete and doorways that were empty rectangles with no door attached. Outside the buildings, people went about their business. Some hurried down the road, others talked to one another. Groups of children in ripped-up clothes asked passing people for money.

As the buildings increased in number, the traffic slowed to a standstill. The truck juddered, and beneath us we felt the motion in the engine slowly grinding to a halt. George was shouting, "CLUTCH DOWN! CLUTCH DOWN!" but I had the clutch to the floor and the engine cut out anyway. I tried the ignition and the engine made one slow gurgle, then went quiet. I turned the key a few more times but the engine stayed silent. I put the handbrake on, and we sat there, not speaking. Cars behind us began to honk their horns, then gave up and moved around us.

George got out of the car, opened the hood of the truck and started tinkering with the engine. He told me that we'd only get started with a jump, so I got out and tried to flag a car down. When it gets dark in Kenya, it happens in minutes, and I didn't think we'd have more than a couple of hours until sunset. I kept an eye on my watch as I waved at the passing cars.

Finally, a sleek black car with a two-foot neon crucifix on its roof pulled in behind us, and two young men in smart black suits and sunglasses got out, asking if they could help. They tried to give us a jump, but their battery didn't have enough power.

"We will get our friend to come and help you with his truck," one of the guys said. "He lives near here. But this is an unsafe area." He pointed to a mass of grey huts half a mile from the roadside. "That area over there is a slum. You shouldn't be here when it gets dark."

True to their word, it was not long before their friend turned up and got our truck started again. But after less than a mile, our saviours had left us, and the car cut out once more. We were stranded for a second time. It was nearly half five by this time. I asked George what time he thought it got dark.

"I don't know," he said. "Six? Maybe half six?"

On the road, children weaved through the slow traffic, begging for money at car windows. They had no shoes, and their clothes were ragged. Some of them were drinking from bottles of cough medicine. Others were inhaling solvents from plastic bags. A couple of them tried pulling on the door handles.

"Hey!" said George. "What are you doing?" They walked away nonchalantly.

We called our mechanic in the city, and he told us to get to a garage. He said we would be able to get a tow from a garage to his place, where he would be able to have a look at the truck for us.

"Just get to a garage," he said. "It's usually the safest place to be, because you're in a dodgy area, you know. You shouldn't be there when it gets dark."

The concerned voice of the mechanic hung in the truck with us after the phone call. Between watching the children slowly gather around our car and glancing at the darkening sky, something inside me began to falter.

"They probably have older friends, George," I said, nodding at the now sizable group of street children on the road around us. "They might be getting them now. Let's go and get a bus. To a hotel somewhere. We can just leave the truck." I never looked at George as I spoke. I kept my eyes on the street outside.

"I'm not leaving my fucking truck," said George.

One of the boys was pleading with us through the window to give him money so that he could go to school. "Please, I don't want to live here, I just need some money," he said, his voice muffled by the glass. "I want to go to school but I don't have money." He had a bottle of cough medicine in his hand. His face was very close to the window, but his eyes weren't focussed on anything.

"Let's just actually think for a minute," said George. "Don't get stressed."

"Maybe we should turn these kids into friends rather than make them into enemies," I said. "They might know where a petrol station is."

"Maybe they can help push us to a petrol station," said George.

I started scrambling out of the truck and George said, "Make a deal first. Agree on a price first."

I climbed out.

"Hey man, do you know where a garage is? For our truck?" I asked the boy closest to my door, the one with the cough medicine. "Where we can buy some petrol?" He said he did and pointed to where we needed to go.

"OK," I said. "Do you want to make some money? If you and your friends over there help us push our truck to the petrol station, we'll pay you some money. What's your price? How much?"

He considered for a moment. "Fifteen shillings," he said.

"OK, that's fine. Fifteen shillings each, no problem."

"No, thirty shillings."

"That's fine. Can you explain to your friends what we need to do?"

We all started pushing. George helped us get it rolling and then jumped into the cab to steer. As we moved into the city, the town got busier, and people walking on the pavement stopped to watch the spectacle: Two red-bearded white men manually moving their broken truck down a busy road with a bunch of street kids. As we moved, more kids joined in and helped us push, as well as one adolescent with a shaved head and an air of authority.

"What is the problem with your truck?" he asked me.

"We don't know," I said. "We need to get it to a garage. Are we going the right way to get to one?"

"Yes, we're going the right way."

The adolescent helped push the truck from behind and organised the younger boys around the truck, getting an even amount on each side. When we came to a junction, he shouted to me which way we needed to go, and I passed it on to George so he could steer the truck in the right direction. It was hectic, and amidst all the chaos the truck rolled over my foot, but I barely felt it.

The street was dry, and you could hear our feet scraping through the grit and dust that coated the ground. The row of four-storey buildings on either side of the road was overwhelming after the open savannah we had passed through. The front of each building had a coloured sign with a business name on it, and as we moved, the signs came together like a mosaic in the adrenaline that blended everything. The truck pulled us as much as we pushed it. On the winding streets it felt like we were a marble on a marble run. We took a sharp corner and the adolescent with the shaved head ordered some of the younger boys to move onto the side I was on to help make the manoeuvre. I turned around and looked at them behind me. The boy closest to me was probably only eleven or twelve. He was wearing an expression of absolute conviction.

We came to the top of a hill, and the road stretched out in front of us. Someone shouted that the petrol station was on the left at the bottom of the hill. We picked up speed as we descended, and I saw the opening of the garage and a few red fuel pumps. As we rolled in, two men dressed like mechanics came to guide us. We pushed the truck to the far side of the court and George got out of the cab. We both shook hands with a few of the boys who had helped us. I went back to the truck and dug around in the back of the cab to get some cash, then walked over to the office that sat at the back, behind the petrol pumps.

The office had a plush, red interior. There was a desk with a man and a woman sitting at it, both dressed in smart clothes. The woman wouldn't look at me, but her colleague smiled and said hello. He looked amused. I asked him if I could change the three thousand shillings I had in cash into the smallest notes they could manage. He chuckled as he counted out the change. "They will have your pockets turned out," he said.

When I went back outside, there was a crowd around George, and I could hear raised voices and George saying, "We only made a deal to pay three of you." The adolescent with the shaved head turned to me as I walked over, his face screwed up in frustration.

"Tell your friend," he said. "He says he won't pay us."

"What's your name?" I asked him.

"Denis," he said. We interlocked our hands.

"I'm Jay," I said. "Denis, I've got some money for you, but you need to promise that you'll share it with all the people who helped us, and make sure that everyone understands that there's no more money."

"OK, that's fine," he said, and I took the broken-up three thousand shillings from my pocket and put it in his hand. He looked at the money with raised eyebrows, and for a second the rhythm of his authority was disrupted; I hadn't done it on purpose, but it was much more than he had expected. There was a moment of quiet while Denis considered the money and the group of boys around him. The boys all watched him.

"Jay," he said, smiling, "let me be the first to share with you," and he took the first note from the pile I had given him and slapped it back into my hand. The group of boys around us started laughing and talking to one another. It was almost a cheer. After a few more handshakes and a promise to return later to check that we were OK, Denis walked away, guiding the group of younger boys out with him.

One of the mechanics came over and told us that they had called a tow truck. George offered me a cigarette and I took it. We walked away from the petrol pumps to smoke. We lit our cigarettes and hugged, slapping each other's backs.

"Fucking hell," I said.

We started laughing, and I felt tears collecting at the bottom of my eyes. Abruptly, I was struck with a feeling of overwhelming love for George, and for Denis, and for all the boys who had helped push the truck, as well as the men who had given us the jump-start. I loved everybody. I grabbed George and hugged him again. When we let go of one another, George looked over at the truck and started laughing again. I did too. I couldn't help it.

As I smoked, I looked out at the city and could see the sun setting behind the rooftops of the buildings in front of us, and together we stood watching the sunset that we had been so scared of just twenty minutes before, with its gentle fingers of orange and white spreading through the dust and the heat.

8

A Grape Harvest

The First Trip—One

When I rolled into Lyon and got off the train that linked the airport to the city, I was homesick and out of my depth and felt so uneasy that I decided to find a base for myself as quickly as possible. Speaking eight disconnected words of French to a young couple, I managed to get myself directed to a hotel and went straight there. It was the first time I had stayed alone in a hotel, and I didn't know a thing about hostels, or anything for that matter, so I just paid the forty euros that the clerk was asking for, even though I couldn't really afford it, and then I had a drink downstairs in the bar, which was a bleak and sterile place with red walls and six-foot plastic lamps. There was no one to talk to.

After a few beers, I felt more confident and went out again, walking back to the train station and drinking a few more pints in a pub next door while making eyes at a woman wearing a wedding ring who was twenty years older than me and also drinking alone. Nothing happened, so I went back to the hotel bar, where I drank some more. Then I went upstairs and fell onto the double bed, crying under the amber lighting for no particular reason before eventually falling asleep. That night I had a dream that some men had stolen the watch my dad had given me, and I was shouting the word *'No'* over and over at them. When I woke in the morning, my throat was sore and I'd lost my voice, so I knew I'd been shouting in my sleep.

———

I'd finished my college course just a few months before, and over the summer was working in a bookshop in Devon to save some money. I'd managed to scramble together a bit of cash and decided to go abroad with it. The decision had been knee-jerk. My education was coming to an end, and I had exactly zero plans for the future. At that time, I just couldn't get a grip on things. Although they didn't say it, I knew that my parents were concerned about me.

One evening, I had asked my sister if Mum and Dad were worrying about what I was going to do when I finished college. She hesitated as she considered her answer, and her silence told me everything. I was so pissed off that I left the room before she had a chance to reply. But really, I didn't need to ask people what they thought. I understood my situation. Our family friends had kids my age who were all on their way to university, while I could barely find it in me to turn up to college. And whenever I did, I was stoned. After storming out, I made up my mind that no matter what happened, I wasn't going to be left behind. I knew everyone had been expecting me to end up getting trapped there, in the village where I'd grown up, just like the sad bastards in the village pub, but I wouldn't let it happen. After the conversation with my sister, I started making plans to leave the country the next day.

Resources were going to be tight. To help me out, one of my colleagues at the bookshop had found me a job at a vineyard in France through a childhood friend, who had moved to the Beaujolais region of France and lived in the same little village as a local winemaker. Her friend had organised it and gave me step-by-step instructions that directed me from the train station in Lyon to the vineyard. After my night in the hotel, I set off early, walking while holding the handwritten guidance in front of me like a map.

Following the instructions, I took a train to Villefranche, where I bought a bus ticket from a kiosk in a small brick building to my stop at the far end of the Beaujolais region. I had to show the man in the kiosk the piece of paper with my directions, as I couldn't pronounce what was written on it. Once I had my ticket, I went outside again and waited for several hours smoking cigarettes and drinking Coca-Cola, feeling hungover. The little bus station and the street around it slowly filled up with other people, many arriving with rucksacks, but some carrying suitcases, while others were holding tents. Everyone was under thirty. I assumed they were seasonal workers like me, coming to pick grapes. When the bus arrived, we all piled on, and it took us through Beaujolais country, which at that time of year was composed of dried-out limestone hills with rows of dark-green vines.

The bus driver had promised to tell me when he reached my stop, and we had just passed through a little town and were in the middle of nowhere when he stopped and called over to me. I got off and the bus pulled away.

I was left standing on the side of the road not really sure where I was. I started walking anyway. The sun was like a furnace, and there were no trees around me, or anything to shelter under except grape vines that were half my height, so I carried on walking, wondering about sunstroke. I started to think that maybe I should try lying down between the rows of vines and waiting until the heat had passed before walking any further when a car pulled up. The woman driving asked where I was going, and when I named the vineyard, she opened her door for me to get in. She drove the distance that would have taken me hours to walk, travelling in silence because she spoke no English and I spoke no real French.

We pulled off the main road, which held no traffic other than the car we were in, and rattled down a steep gravel path. We approached a tall stone farmhouse and stopped, and the woman motioned for me to get out. She went to the boot, where she pulled out my bag and hoisted it onto her shoulder like it didn't weigh a thing, carrying it over to my side of the car. She pushed it into my chest, and then we walked down the rest of the gravel slope together. Soon we came to the farmhouse, which had a veranda with a group of people standing on it. The lady introduced me and pointed to the group in a gesture that I took to mean that I should join them. Then she walked around to the other side of the building and disappeared out of view.

When I approached the group, I was offered a round of hands to shake. Mostly the group was young people in their early twenties, but there was also a man in his forties with long, red-blonde hair and beard, and an older, fat, pig-faced man who sneered as I greeted him. There was also a middle-aged couple who were both short and fat and plain, like male and female versions of each other. One of the younger men, also with long hair, shook my hand and introduced himself in English as Hugo. He had a thick French accent.

"How old are you?" Hugo asked.

"Nineteen," I said.

"Nineteen?"

"Yes."

He gave me a beer, I offered him a cigarette, and we went out and sat with another young Frenchman called Luc, who was a friend of Hugo's. We all smoked. Hugo and Luc were both in a band that played sludge metal, and so we talked about that. After a little while the vineyard owner, Martin, came and greeted us. He was lean and Roman-nosed, and his skin was tanned olive. You could tell by his frayed collar and dust-covered trousers that he was wearing the clothes he worked in. He shook my hand.

"Comment ça va?" he asked.

"Ça va."

Martin smiled and went to greet a few of the others. Then we were all invited down to the front of the house, where we stood in a big circle and drank an aperitif, a small glass of sweet liquor I had never had before. Words were said and jokes were made, and I could tell that a lot of the people there had known Martin for a long time.

After a while, Martin took us through a pair of big wooden doors leading to the ground floor that was dark and cool, with stone floors and long stretches of wooden tables and benches. We were served a plate of salad, followed by spaghetti Bolognese, then a dessert, followed by a cheese board that sat on the table with some fresh bread. There was also endless wine. When we were finished, we went back up to the veranda. The pig-faced man took some of the bottles with him.

The next day we got to work, and the routine we settled into would not change for the rest of the grape harvest, which the other workers called a vendange. We would wake at six, not long after the sun had come up, go downstairs to the dining room and eat breakfast, which was cereal or bread or croissants or fruit, and drink coffee or hot chocolate from a bowl. Then we would pile into Martin's van and his brother's car and drive to a spot somewhere in the rolling hills, where we would be allocated a row of vines in which to harvest the grapes. If you finished your row early, it was customary to help another worker, starting at the top of their vine while they worked from the bottom until you both met in the middle. We were given a choice of two tools: a pair of secateurs or a serpette, which was a hooked blade like a billhook but thinner. You'd wrap the serpette around the vine you were trying to cut and pull it while twisting at the same time. I happened to pick up the serpette, so that was what I used for the next twelve days. The hardest part was that the rows started low down and weren't quite as tall as a grown man, so I had to stoop to reach most of the grapes, which hurt my back. The experienced workers moved along the vine while crouching, but I couldn't get the hang of it.

We would have a break in the morning at around ten, where we would eat salami, cheese and bread that was passed around in big plastic boxes, and drink coffee or water from thermos flasks; there was also wine, which some of the older workers drank mixed with water, even at ten in the morning. Then we would all smoke. Sometimes Martin would pass around his packet of Marlboro Lights, but mostly I rolled my own. Then we would get back to it before lunch, which we'd have in three courses back at the house in the cool, stone-floored dining room.

After lunch, we'd head back out to pick grapes again until

around six in the evening, with another short break out near the vines to rest our backs before the final row. When we got back to the house, we'd have another meal, meaning we ate five times a day. When we had finished eating our evening meal, Hugo, Luc and I would drive out to the nearest town in Hugo's little red Peugeot and buy some beers and tobacco, and then spend the evening drinking and listening to music. We drank Kronenbourg, which was the cheapest beer we could find in the one shop that was in the town. We kept it in a box under the table on the veranda to shelter it from the sun. When Hugo took the beers out for us to drink, he'd hold the bottle at the base so as not to obscure the label, and steady it at the neck with his other hand, raising it up like it was a bottle of good wine being presented to us at a restaurant. Luc would ask things like, "Is that the Sixty-Four? A good vintage?"

I spent most of my time with Luc and Hugo, but the rest of the group were generally accommodating. Over the course of the two weeks, I learnt to pick out individual French words but never progressed much further than that. I'd listen in on conversations, though, and felt that I got a good feel of what the members of the group were like.

The only member who didn't seem to want me there was the pig-faced man. He was a police officer. He would crack jokes at the expense of the only black employee, and once I heard him call him *nègre*. Sometimes he'd crack jokes at my expense too. On my first night, he told Hugo and Luc that they should avoid me, as the English were the cause of the swine flu pandemic. Hugo and Luc told me that the police in France would sometimes drive through the black and Eastern European neighbourhoods and shoot rubber bullets at children from their moving cars.

Not everyone could take the work. There was a young man called Dominique, who wore a crucifix around his neck, which a few times I saw him kissing before we started work. He was kind and talkative but overconfident, and on the first day did press-ups publicly in the lounge of the workers' quarters during our break. Once, after work, he invited me to his car to listen to Biggie Smalls, rapping along to the part about cum sluts and whores.

Dominique's work began to falter after the first couple of days, and Martin took him to one side and talked to him. When Dominique wouldn't look him in the eye, Martin snapped at him, gesturing at his own eyes with a rigid index finger. A few days later, Dominique left the vineyard. It wasn't clear to me if it was his decision or Martin's. Before he left, Dominique came to say goodbye. "My honour is hurt," he said. "I've failed."

It appeared that there were two types of vendange. We were doing the family-oriented version, which meant getting fed well with good food and sleeping at night in a house. The work was backbreaking, but most of the people there were doing it as a holiday from their normal jobs. The middle-aged couple had done it every year for the past twelve years—always with Martin and his wife, Lucie. The other workers said Martin and Lucie were like family. One evening, Martin took us out to a local bar, where he filled the table with bottles of wine. He just kept setting them on the table. Then we all went back and ate at his brother's house, where the atmosphere was like a Christmas Day dinner.

The other kind of vendange meant sleeping in a field in your own tent, and maybe getting less in the way of free meals but making more money. We saw these work crews as we drove to get beers—a mixture of students, Roma families and New Age travellers. One evening, as we drove past a campsite used by these other grape pickers, we passed a girl who was maybe even younger than me, with ragged trainers and olive skin. She had dark brown eyes. Our eyes met as we drove by, and then she walked away. It felt like she wanted me to follow her. I would have followed her anywhere. I watched her in the rearview mirror. Hugo must have seen me looking.

"Jay, be careful, there are a lot of unshaven girls here," he said.

At the end of the twelve days, we waited on the stone forecourt in front of the dining room while Martin called us in one by one, paying us individually. When it was my turn to go and see him, Martin had my payment laid out in cash, knowing I wasn't going home until the end of the summer and so couldn't cash a cheque. He gave me one thousand four hundred euros, along with a cardboard container that held three bottles of his wine. When Martin had counted out my money, he shook my hand and looked me in the eye. Lucie came over from the back of the room, where she had been cutting potatoes, and shook my hand too. I was too young to grasp it fully, but I knew that Martin and Lucie liked me, and by the atmosphere or perhaps just intuition, I was in some way aware that they were shaking my hand in accordance with a way of life that was slowly being forgotten; a way of life that was leaving the world, one closed-down family farm at a time, and that I was privileged to have lived within it for a while.

Hugo, Luc and I climbed into Hugo's little red Peugeot and drove to their hometown, Chambéry, on the Italian border. They said I could hitchhike or get a train from there. As we drove, Luc rolled a spliff and passed it back to me, and Hugo played *The End* by The Doors, which was the first time I'd heard it. As we drove, Luc put his hand out of the window and played with the air with his fingers.

9

And the Dogs Hated Our Walking Poles

The Walk to Spain — Four

I found Bordeaux to be an extremely grand city. I arrived in the town early and found a bar with a seating area overlooking a promenade, where I drank coffee and smoked. I got talking with a ghost writer, a slim man in his forties who gave me a list of wines to try while in the city, as well as a list of French authors I should read. On that list was *The Plague* by Albert Camus. The ghost writer said, "When you finish reading this book, you are a different person." When I went to leave, he insisted on paying for my drinks, saying he was acting as an ambassador for the people of Bordeaux. In return, I gave him a book of Wordsworth's poetry I had carried with me from England.

I found my way to an Internet café. Using the Couchsurfing website, I made contact with a young couple called Juliette and Tom, who met me in the city centre, gave me a quick tour and also offered me a bed for the night. Both of them were planning a walking holiday and asked me questions about what I carried with me and what I ate each day. Juliette's parents were from

Southern France and still spoke Occitan as their mother tongue.

Together we walked through a market, and as the days were becoming brighter with summer approaching, I decided to buy a hat, one with a plump top, like a beret, but with a peak. Juliette said it was a traditional hat from Nîmes. I stayed in the town one more day, enjoying the sunshine, and then I walked out of the city, heading south, my new cap pulled down to shield my eyes from the spring sunlight.

A pilgrim I met not long out of Nantes, who had done the Camino before, had warned me of Landes de Gascogne Regional Natural Park, which came after Bordeaux. She described it as a week's walk through a commercial pine forest that supported almost no life other than insects that bite. I hadn't long left the city before I got a taste of it.

The Landes de Gascogne, or at least the part that I passed through, was a vast sprawl of pine trees lined up in uniform, man-made rows, which occasionally opened into patches of felled woodland. Underfoot, the soil was seventy per cent sand, which made it hard to walk. The ground in the areas where the trees had been cleared was almost always scorched. I guessed that the ground was burnt as part of the clearing process once the trees had been felled. Black ash mixed into white sand, making grey dirt that clung to my boots and marked my clothes. Just as I'd been told, the ground was alive with insects that bit me when I sat to eat or rest. I ate standing up if I couldn't find something to sit down on. I heard no birds for the most part, aside from the occasional cuckoo. But I did see deer. Because of the straight rows of trees and the wide gaps between them, the deer couldn't shelter, meaning that I could watch them clearly as they moved around, sometimes for minutes at a time.

And the people who lived in Gascogne were some of the best I'd met since I'd left England. A lumberjack who I asked for directions helped me by drawing maps in the sand, and when he was done, his eyes lit up when he remembered that he had some coffee he could share with me. He showed me to a felled log that was as good as a bench. We sat together and he asked me questions about my trip while I drank the coffee he had given me, which was sweet with the three sugar cubes he had piled into it. His face was earnest and enthusiastic, childlike against his huge, thickset body and red workman's dungarees.

For the rest of my time in the park, the locals greeted me warmly and with open sincerity. They all wanted to help me out. One morning, while I packed my tent, a local man came to me and asked if I liked coffee. I told him I did and walked off, only realising later that he was probably offering me a cup. For the next week, I felt sick with guilt every time I thought of it.

It took me around three days to pass through the park. I knew from my guidebooks that from the end of the reserve, I would have just one more short leg of maybe three or four days before I reached Saint-Jean-Pied-de-Port, where there would be many more people walking the Camino. I was ready for their company. The burn of solitude was becoming too much, despite any acclimatisation to being alone that I had gone through. I walked quickly, covering as much ground as I could each day, eager for the company of others. Since leaving England three months earlier, I had frequently gone for days without speaking to anyone; on a few occasions, I had gone a week. I was aware that I was speaking to myself more frequently. Sometimes I'd verbalise my thoughts and respond to them. Other times I would daydream about past or imagined conversations, and I would mouth the words being said in them to myself. I was wearing a digital watch that let out two short beeps every hour, and by the end of my time in Gascogne, I had gotten into the habit of beeping back to the watch merrily, as if the watch and I were sharing a joke.

———

I was passing through a town called Labouheyre, a day's walk from the end of the park. The day was boiling hot, and I was looking for somewhere that would sell me a Coke that I could sip in the shade. I came to a crossroads and was examining a road sign, looking for the best route south, when I was approached by a red-faced man. He had white hair and walked with a golden walking stick. His stomach bulged under his T-shirt, which was tucked into a pair of ancient corduroy slacks. Over the top of the T-shirt he wore a pair of red braces holding his trousers up. He asked me if I was a pilgrim, and when I told him that I supposed that I was, he started speaking to me in incomprehensible French while gesturing erratically with his hands, his voice dry and manic. I couldn't understand what he was saying, but I could tell that he wanted me to follow him. We walked together to the other side of Labouheyre, and he moved with surprising energy despite his age, always rambling in a stream of bewildering French. As he talked to me, he frothed at the mouth but didn't seem to notice. The froth clung around his lips, occasionally spraying forward when he laughed.

We got to his house, which was a sparse cottage—more like a shack. It had a barren but clinging smell, like wax mixed with stale urine. It reminded me of the house of a childhood friend whose mother had been a heavy alcoholic. The Frenchman pointed to a chair, where I sat down. He went about taking

131

spaghetti from a huge, uncovered pot that sat on the dilapidated stove and transferred it into a bowl, then reheated it for me in the microwave, all the while still talking to me. After the microwave had pinged, he gave me the bowl. The spaghetti tasted good. I realised that I didn't particularly give a shit about the hygiene of the place. While I ate, he showed me photos of him with other pilgrims who had passed through the town. He showed me postcards from Santiago de Compostela too, sent by previous pilgrims as thanks for his hospitality while on their walk. When I finished eating, he reheated some coffee for us and put some cognac in it.

Once I had finished the coffee, I thanked him and said that it was time for me to get back on the road. I stood up like a man with a purpose, clapping my hands and rubbing them together. I told him I was eager to walk, and that since it was only midday, that was what I was going to do. This sparked his erratic talking again, and he asked me to follow him as he walked to the other side of his little cottage to show me to a spare bedroom with a made-up bed. The room smelt damp despite the heat outside. The bedclothes had been left in place for so long that they had moulded themselves to the shape of the mattress.

The man was still rambling and pointing at the bed, his words coming at me like a machine gun, each sentence punctuated with manic laughter. I knew that he wanted me to stay; not because he wanted to help me, but because he wanted to add me to his collection and show my photo to the next pilgrim to pass through the town. I told him in my clearest French that it was not the time for me to stop walking and that I didn't want to lose half a day's walk by stopping early. He started to protest but I cut him off, shook his hand and walked away. He still managed to shove his address into my pocket as I walked out the door, telling me to send him a postcard once I had finished my walk. I got out and started moving, but for the rest of the day I expected him to turn up wherever I was.

The next day, after finally coming to the end of the park and camping the night a few kilometres south of the forest, I made it to Dax, the last major town I would pass through before the Pyrenees mountains, which marked the border between France and Spain. While in the town centre I made a trip to the shops for some basic supplies, stopping in a gift shop to buy a few postcards. As Amelia's birthday was a week later, I wanted to buy a card for her, too, but the selection of birthday cards was tiny, and mostly in French. In the end I opted for one with a polar bear on the front, which was probably aimed at children. It was a pathetic effort. I had left it too late to send a present, and I felt guilty sending the first card I happened to come across, but it was that or nothing at all. Amelia and I hadn't had a proper conversation since Nantes.

Among the postcards I had bought, there was one showing a row of ladies kneeling naked on the beach, their breasts covered by their arms as they crouched. I wouldn't have even looked at it a few months earlier, but after two months of virtually no contact with Amelia, or any other women, I gave in to inevitability and bought it, doing my best to make proud eye contact with the lady behind the counter, who I had held a polite conversation with ten minutes earlier. Then I went to a café and asked the woman working there to fill my water bottle, the same plastic evian bottle I had been using since I'd left Devon. By that point it was a disfigured mess. It had been crushed so many times that the light refracted off each crease, making it look almost white rather than see-through.

133

I spent the night camping just outside Dax and followed it with a day walking through vibrant, green countryside, finding my way to a hostel for pilgrims in a town called Sorde-l'Abbaye just before dark. The next morning, I set off early again, and before lunch I had entered a new terrain that was completely unprecedented to me: rolling hills with delicate woodlands and wild meadows with bright, green grass speckled with wildflowers. It was the kind of scenery that makes you want to do more than just look at it; looking's not enough. You want to somehow get involved in it too; take a running jump and bounce around on it. Behind the hills I could see the Pyrenees.

I was slowly rising upwards. The winding path I was following stretched out in front of me and receded into the distance. During the Spanish Civil War, the Pyrenees had been the point of access for foreign idealists coming to fight against the military dictator, General Francisco Franco. Among them had been the writer Laurie Lee. Not long before I'd left England, I'd read everything Laurie Lee had written, including the journey he claimed to have made across the mountains in December 1937 to join the fight. Apparently, he got caught in a snowstorm halfway across, and he made it sound like it was nearly the end of him. Lee's story had made an impression on me, and the Pyrenees were one of the few parts of the journey I had preconceptions about before I left. I'd thought about them with a mixture of fear and excitement since leaving home.

But the inhospitable landscape that Lee promised never quite showed itself. The day was warm, visibility was good and the road I walked on was well tarmacked. Occasionally, I passed through small hamlets, with kids playing outside and parents working in their gardens, and I was in turn passed by the occasional dilapidated postal van. The people I came across were polite and kind to me, but the limitless hospitality I had experienced in Gascogne was gone. When I approached residents to ask for water, they spoke to me in French and filled my bottle without hesitation, but made no conversation. When they spoke to one another, it was in a language completely new to me, short and clipped and with rolling consonants. I guessed that they were speaking Euskara, which meant I was in Basque Country, and that I would be approaching the Spanish border probably by the end of the day. I was so close I could feel it. I decided to put it all in to make the most ground possible.

It was probably during this one last push that I broke a small bone in my left foot. The trail leading me to the mountains was beautiful, but the well-tarmacked road proved hard on my feet. On that last day in France, as I walked the better part of thirty miles, something in my foot gave out. The pain surfaced not long after lunch and nagged at me for the rest of the day, forcing me to favour my right leg as I walked. But I kept going. For most people walking the Camino de Santiago, Saint-Jean-Pied-de-Port was the start. I knew that the town would be filled with people starting their pilgrimage, and after the months I'd spent alone, I couldn't stop thinking about making it there and meeting other people. I was obsessed with the idea of it.

And so, I limped into Saint-Jean-Pied-de-Port, reeking, two stone lighter than when I'd left England, and hungry for conversation. I was stunned by the sheer volume of pilgrims. The roads were blocked with cars trying to negotiate their way around the little mountain town, and the first hostels I came to all had queues outside. Despite this, tradition still clearly stood, and the official religious albergue listed in my guidebook didn't open its doors until half nine and locked them at midnight. They wouldn't let you back in if you were out any later than that. I decided to walk further into the town centre, where I found another small albergue with no queue and took my first shower of the week.

After washing, I put my dirty clothes back on and headed out to find somewhere that would sell me a cheap meal, although it seemed that cheap meals did not exist in that town. In the end I settled for an overpriced pork dish, followed by a single beer, in an overpriced restaurant, watching the other pilgrims around me arguing with one another over parking, each kitted out in a thousand pounds of trekking gear. I would have liked to drink more, but I couldn't afford it.

I spent the night in a room with two Dutchmen—a father of around seventy, and his son, perhaps forty. The son saw me limping and gave me some high-dose ibuprofen that his wife, a nurse, had given him.

"I just sent her an SMS saying that I had given you four," he said, giggling. His dad and I giggled with him.

"And now she has messaged back saying, 'No, no! That's too much!'"

"You should tell her not to worry because he's sleeping good!" said the father, and we all laughed again, and I went to sleep happy because I was enjoying their company, and because I'd made it to the border and could still laugh with these men, despite the months of solitude and my new habit of talking to myself. I hadn't gone insane after all.

In the morning, a group of Norwegians were eating their breakfast at the table next to me and the two Dutchmen. After hearing that I had walked from England, they came to talk to me; only they didn't speak much English, and what resulted was a well-meaning but confused conversation in which the only thing they truly learnt was my name. After breakfast, I left the two Dutchmen and threw myself into the climb towards the heart of the mountains, up a steep, dusty path that was populated by a stream of pilgrims. The line of pilgrims was like a fat-tailed snake: thick at the bottom, where everyone started together, and then it thinned as the difficulty of the climb cut divisions into it.

I walked as I had learnt to walk on the Coast Path, with my rucksack pulled tight to my back and rocking my stiff upper body back and forth rigidly, propelling myself up the hill in a kind of Newtonian spasticity. I passed the Norwegians, who shouted, "Jay!" and raised their hands in the air as I walked past them. I raised mine back. I noticed that everyone had small bags, carrying just enough for staying in the hostels that were supposed to be omnipresent from here on. Most of the walkers had plush, new hiking gear. Mine was ragged, slept in and stained by a winter's mud.

I stopped to drink some water and smoke a cigarette, asking another walker for a light. His name was Javier, a six-foot-three-inch Spaniard with broad shoulders. We smoked together, and he introduced me to a group of six other ragtag Europeans who had all met for the first time that morning. I could tell that Javier was the glue of the group. Together, the eight of us crossed into Spain. There was nothing marking the transition across borders other than a stone on the ground that had "Welcome to Spain" painted on it. Javier took a shine to me and bought me tapas and drinks in a little mountain bar when we stopped for lunch.

When the day's walk was over, we stayed in a huge, ancient albergue that looked almost like a castle nestled into the mountain, with towering white walls. The side of the building had rows of square windows running across it. The grounds around the building were uneven, swelling into little mounts, and at points the albergue seemed almost submerged in the grassy hills that surrounded it. Inside, the dormitories were colossal, with probably a hundred people to each one. The dorm we settled into was a giant open space, with a curved ceiling held up by twenty-foot wooden beams.

The beds were grouped in twos and had a low wooden wall around each one, almost like a cubicle. The bed next to me was occupied by a Spanish woman, and when we rose to set off the next morning, she gave me a filthy look as she packed up her belongings. Later that day we encountered her again, and Javier spoke to her briefly in Spanish, breaking out into laughter halfway through the conversation. After the lady had left, Javier said to me that when he told her I had walked all the way to Spain from England, she had replied, "Thank God. I didn't think it was possible to smell so bad after just one day."

We walked for three days through the Spanish countryside, passing beautiful mountain towns dotted with stone bridges and fields that were home to sand-coloured cows with twelve-inch horns. At the end of the third day, I separated from the group with Ben, another Englishman who had recently left his long-term boyfriend. We wanted to try and get the walk done a bit faster than the rest. Together, we passed through Pamplona, a worn-down and hostile town with socialist and Basque separatist graffiti sprayed onto the cash machines, and where, like most Spanish towns at that time, you saw thirty empty building sites for every one still up and running.

As we walked, Ben and I talked. He'd studied physics at university, and after he'd graduated, he worked as a banker in London, where he met a colleague who eventually became his partner, and then his ex. Ben had never really felt that banking was for him, though, and after a few years he moved into teaching. He asked a lot of questions, could hold a conversation on pretty much anything and wasn't afraid to challenge me if he disagreed with something. He disapproved of my cigarette smoking and coffee drinking. One lunchtime, we had a sandwich in a café, and when we had finished eating, Ben started quizzing me on why I wouldn't try quitting smoking. I couldn't be bothered with it and went outside and sparked up. He finished his juice and joined me outside a few minutes later. We started walking.

"You were getting a bit edgy then, before you had your cigarette," he said.

"No, I wasn't," I said. "Have you ever smoked?"

"Not really. I've always been really sporty. I never understood why I'd want to do something that would make playing sports harder."

"What about coffee then? Why don't you drink coffee?"

"Again, I just never really started. When I was a child, my mum told me that tea and coffee were bad for me. I asked if they were bad for adults too, and when I was told they were, I made a decision not to drink them. I just never started drinking them."

"But when you're a kid, didn't that make you determined to start drinking them? My mum used to say the same thing and it didn't stop me wanting them."

"I don't know, I don't remember that part. This was thirty years ago. My parents didn't smoke, though, which makes you less likely to smoke, don't you think? Does your dad smoke?"

"He did, but he quit a while ago now."

"Does he know you smoke?"

"I think so. When I was in school, he found my cigarettes at least once. And there were a few occasions when I knew he could tell I was stoned."

"When was that? When you were a teenager?"

"Yeah, at some point before I moved out."

"How old were you when you moved out?"

"Nineteen."

"And you moved to Bristol?"

"First I went to France and worked on a vineyard, did a bit of backpacking around Europe, and then I moved to Bristol when I got back."

"What did your parents think about the travelling and weed smoking?"

"I think they supported the travelling, my mum particularly."

"That's good."

"It's amazing, really. I dropped by to visit a friend a few days before I set off, and his mum asked about the walk. When I gave her the details, I could see how nervous it made her. I'd never even thought about it until then, but I'm sure my mum felt nervous too, but she didn't show it. She probably didn't want to put me off."

"What about your dad? Was he nervous?"

"Yeah, but he couldn't really hide it."

We talked about how Ben's ex always had to do everything the hardest way possible and the strain this put them both under, and about how he kept saying things were going to change, but they never did. I told Ben about Amelia, who had been texting that day to tell me she had booked a flight to Santiago, and how it would be the first time seeing each other in months. Ben asked me a lot of questions about my dad. I told him about the time I was arrested. When I was released the next day, my dad wouldn't come to pick me up, even though the police had taken my shoes as evidence and no buses were running. Although in the end he did pay for a taxi for me.

"I don't know why he wouldn't get me, really," I said. "Or why he eventually preferred to get me a taxi, which was much more expensive. I think he was both angry and worried."

"You might find, as you get older, your role in the relationship changes, and you might take the lead," said Ben. "A little while ago I started planning walking holidays with my dad, and they've been really good for us. He's really enjoyed them. We've both really enjoyed them."

Together, Ben and I walked through four days of Spanish countryside and an agricultural region where the plants were green-blue. They were so colourful they looked almost unnatural to me. The earth underneath the plants was a rich orange. The whole landscape looked alien. I wondered if there was a mineral present in the soil that was acting as a dye. We then reached La Rioja, which was hilly and rugged and filled with low vines marking the hills like contour lines on a map. There was also a drinking fountain for pilgrims that offered red wine or water.

We filled our bottles, one with wine and one with water, and then carried on to Santo Domingo, where we stayed in another religious albergue with a curfew of nine o'clock. Inside the albergue, people slept on the floor of a single open room; it looked like an emptied church. There was a physiotherapist set up in the corner who was checking over walkers' injuries in return for a donation. He was a young man but had a mane of black hair and weather-beaten skin. His eyes were serious and uncompromising. I showed him my foot, and he flexed my toes individually. When I grimaced in pain, he told me that the only thing for it was rest. I asked him about pain relief.

"Yes, you can take something like that, but the pain is talking to you," he said. "If you ignore it, maybe you will hurt your foot more."

"So, I shouldn't take them?" I asked.

"Just don't take them too much. Like once a day. And rest if you can."

I thanked him and asked how much I owed. He said it depended on how much money I had. If I had money, then he'd take fifteen euros, or more, but if I was poor, it was free. I thought about my dwindling cash reserves.

"I'm not that poor," I said.

"I'm poor," he said, his eyes fixed on mine. "I do this because I'm poor."

I gave him ten euros and tried to get some sleep, hoping my foot would thank me for it.

A few days later we passed into Burgos, the first big town since Pamplona, walking along miles of main roads to get there. Some of the roads were half built and closed to cars. Walking along them had a post-apocalyptic feel. We left the town early the next day, catching the morning when it was still damp and you could smell the cold water in the air, and pushed on for another four days. My foot started to nag more and more. Eventually, I had to tell Ben that I didn't think I was going to be able to carry on at the speed we were going. On that same day Ben started to get a cough, which by the end of the day was much worse. At one point he coughed so intensely that he needed to sit to catch his breath. When he had finished coughing, we both agreed there was no point rushing to the end if it was going to make us sick, so Ben changed his plans to fly home from León, rather than

Santiago, which meant we had a week to make the distance if we needed it.

For six days we passed through sparse Spanish farms, deserted back roads and towns that were really just a few stone buildings. The towns were usually home to a single café and a few dogs. Just like in France, the dogs hated walkers. Tied up outside farmhouses, they would bark and snarl at us when they heard the sound of walking poles. As the days moved on, the weather grew cold again, and Ben's summer gear wasn't keeping him warm. He wore my gaiters and a spare pair of thermals I wasn't using, but they weren't quite enough; and on a few occasions, he walked ahead, moving as fast as he could to warm up, then waited in a café for me to arrive as I lumbered along with my heavy backpack.

In the days before we arrived in León, we passed through barren desert and empty towns that felt like they belonged in the Wild West, and we climbed over jarring hills that gave us an eagle-eye view of the trail. Whenever I rose up high enough to get a good vantage point, I watched the pilgrims move along the trail. The huge numbers present in Saint-Jean-Pied-de-Port were gone, and I watched just a few, small clusters making their way through the browned scenery, treading the same path as the previous and following groups, like ants.

———

Seventeen days after crossing over the Spanish border, Ben and I reached León, a city built around a huge square bordered on all four sides by walls of handsome buildings. We found an albergue, and I went to shower. When I came back into the dorm, Ben was talking to a shy and handsome posh lad who introduced himself as Adam. Ben told me they were going to nip out to look at the city, so I left them to it and walked around the town worrying about money because, since I'd been in Spain, I'd not been able to free camp once, so my cash was running out. I wrote some postcards while sitting on a wall in the central square, as I didn't want to pay for a coffee to get access to one of the tables owned by the café. It rained intermittently.

After a few hours I was bored of León and was walking around aimlessly, smoking razor-thin cigarettes to save my tobacco. It was a small town, and it wasn't long before I bumped into Ben again, who was still with his new friend Adam. They were both drunk and told me they had found a place that did a glass of wine and a plate of tapas for a euro each. They took me down an alleyway to a dingy bar with a ceiling so low that I had to stoop to avoid banging my head on the ceiling, and we all had a few drinks and a few plates of tapas. Adam was really drunk. They both were. He was telling us about how he didn't know where to go to university and that his dad had paid for this trip so he could have a think about his future. Twice he knocked a few glasses off the table, and when it was time to run back to the albergue before it closed for the night his flip-flops kept falling off. After we got into bed, Adam went to the bathroom, and I could hear him throwing up. Ben went to help him clean it up.

Ben had decided he was going to fly home the next day. As a favour, he took with him a lot of the gear I didn't need any more: my spare thermals and winter gloves, a jumper and a thermal hat; I would pick them up from him when I finally got home. I didn't want to wait another day in León, and decided to continue walking, leaving Ben in León waiting for his plane. When it was time to go, we hugged goodbye, and I felt that I could cry, as I was losing the first real friend I'd made since setting off from Devon.

I rejoined the Camino. First, I latched onto a hulking German called Max, who had the humour of a depraved squaddie but a heart of pure gold. He found the postcard of the naked women hysterical, and that night, after a few beers, he told me he had been in a terrible motorcycle accident and had to learn to walk and speak for a second time. He said it was like a rebirth, so he was doing the walk to celebrate his new life. After a few days, when Max left to go back to Germany, I walked with some young Austrians and an older German man, communicating by speaking a mix of English, French and German, and sharing our food and anything else we might have that was useful.

The last section of the pilgrimage near Santiago went quickly. As we got closer to the city, the Camino passed through more populated areas, and the last day was spent largely walking around suburbia. Klaus, the older German man, had the day before eaten what he described as the finest cream cake he'd ever encountered. Every café or cake shop we passed, he went in and tried to describe it to whoever was working there, using his broken English, even though the employees only ever spoke Spanish; they never seemed to be able to help him. Not far from the outskirts of Santiago, a woman directed him to a bakery that was away from the trail, tucked in behind the town centre. We all walked fifteen minutes to find it. I waited outside while my two new Austrian friends went in and tried to describe the cake in Spanish, with Klaus standing behind them. After a while, the woman shook her head and Klaus shouted, "Dumme Fotze!" at the top of his lungs, which means 'silly cunt', and then we gave up and headed back to the trail.

A few hours from the city centre, we passed a squat red

building with a neon sign of a heart with an arrow going through it. Two women dressed in short skirts and short jackets stood outside. Their makeup was thick, and they stood very close to one another, almost like lovers. They made eyes at us and wolf-whistled, making my two Austrian friends uncomfortable. We walked on, the women laughing behind us, and went down a labyrinth of descending steps and narrow stone alleyways lined with cobbles smoothed almost flat by the progression of the millions of pilgrims who had walked there before us.

The Santiago de Compostela Cathedral—huge, imposing and ugly, with austere iron railings along its facade—sat in the centre of the square casting a shadow over the plaza in the evening sun. Pilgrims milled around it and took photos next to it. I had walked one thousand six hundred miles to get there, but I didn't want to stay for long. It didn't do much for me. When my companions were ready, we left to find a bed for the night.

That first night in Santiago I went out with the two Austrians and got drunk. They were both devout Catholics, and when I started to get really drunk, they got uncomfortable and left. I stayed out anyway, bouncing from bar to club. My heavy walking boots made it hard to dance, but I carried on. A Spanish guy told me how to say "You have beautiful eyes" in Spanish, and I staggered around the bars saying it to every girl I came into contact with. When all the bars and clubs had closed, I was left wandering the ancient streets looking for a party or a lock-in. Anything. In the early hours of the morning, I found myself standing in the centre of the town, trying to hitchhike back to the girls in short skirts who had wolf-whistled at us when we arrived. A student I had met earlier at a bar came to see if I was alright. Her lips looked engorged, like her makeup was smudged.

I woke up in an unfamiliar bed at ten in the morning. I was supposed to have met Amelia at the airport at half nine. I snuck out the door and walked to my hostel. By the time I got there, my Austrian friends had already left. I never saw them again. I got my stuff together and showered before finding my way to the hotel where Amelia was staying.

Amelia kept telling me how skinny I was. She found my orange beard confusing too. We lay in bed together not speaking. We'd been apart for months. When the paranoia and the booze withdrawal began to seep in, I went out and bought some razors and shaving foam from a nearby corner shop to shave my beard off, hoping that without it I'd be unrecognisable to anyone who had seen me the night before. With a disposable razor, I scraped away the orange hairs that contained the residue of a walk across three countries. When one razor became blunt, I tossed it into the dented bin under the sink and carried on with a fresh one until that went blunt too. Underneath, my face was thin and pale where the beard had been and was a different shape to how I remembered it. When I had finished, I joined Amelia again in our box of a hotel bedroom, with walls that were exactly as tall as they were long and containing only one window, which had a brick wall directly outside it. Under the dim glow of the lightbulb dyed yellow by the lampshade, the room felt like a shipping container.

Amelia asked what I'd done the night before, and I lied and said I'd spent it entirely with my new Austrian friends. Amelia didn't say anything else, but I knew she didn't believe me. As we lay together in bed with neither of us speaking, I looked up at the ceiling, which had a black-speckled stain running across it, and realised that the opportunity for me to be a good man was in the room with us. The silence between us was charged, like the quiet during a play when an actor forgets their line. The seconds stretched out, and I could feel the opportunity to be good was passing, but it was still there. I made an effort to stay aware of it. I kept asking myself, *'Has it gone? No, no, but it will be. What about now? No, still there but further away. And now? What about now?'* Then Amelia stood up and went to the bathroom, and I thought, *'Yeah, now it's gone.'*

I spent a few days in Santiago with Amelia, eating in fast-food restaurants amidst a fog of guilt and suspicion until she left to go home to Birmingham. Then I walked the three days to Cape Finisterre through country paths flanked by imposing green plants that looked almost tropical; it rained continuously. When I arrived at Cape Finisterre, I did it all again—getting drunk with a baby-faced Danish guy I was sharing a hotel room with, and when he got tired and went back to the room, I stayed out, bouncing from club to club.

But Finisterre was not the genteel university town that Santiago was, and in the early morning I found myself sitting in a windowless bar drinking alone. Around me a group of squat, young fishermen tried to control their friend, who was losing his mind in a rage. I couldn't work out how it had all started. He was crying, and the cords stood out on his neck as he strained against his friends. It seemed to go on for hours, and after a while he came at me. I went to break my bottle over his head, but the floor was wet with ice, broken glass and blood, and I slipped, falling well before I made contact with him. He saw what I had tried to do, but his friends didn't, and for a while he went crazier, shouting at me in Spanish before his friends finally managed to bundle him out the door. From outside he hammered on the door, still screaming and crying.

When I got back to the hotel, I had to use the intercom to get the hotelier out of bed so that I could get back in. He looked scandalised. Later in the morning, he said to my Danish companion, "Six in the morning he got home!"

A few months later, I was back in Devon, working in the village pub trying to save up enough money for whatever I was going to do next. Amelia came to visit me. A few days into her visit, I was working a morning shift, and when I got home at lunchtime she was gone. On top of my bed, I found the diary I had written while walking that summer—which included a self-loathing recount of my drunken behaviour in Santiago and everything else I had done or thought about that I wouldn't have wanted Amelia to know. On top of the diary was a letter from her telling me that if I ever wanted to be with anyone after her, I needed a whole new personality first.

I caught a bus to Birmingham and a taxi to Amelia's friend's house, where I found her, tired and puffy faced from crying. We had a two-hour conversation, sitting in her friend's spare bedroom, even though I didn't have anything to say other than to apologise. When the conversation wore itself out, I left and never saw her again.

10

The Woods Near Bardonecchia

The First Trip—Two

Luc and Hugo dropped me off in Chambéry, an alpine town not far from the Italian border. I got out of the car and shook both their hands. "You're a good guy, Jay," Luc said, and for some reason it caught me off guard. It gave me a lump in my throat. I didn't know what to say in reply, so I just said thanks. Then I walked round to the boot of Hugo's little red Peugeot and collected my rucksack and the three bottles of Beaujolais that Lucie and Martin had given me on leaving. I hugged them both, and they drove off, the little red car giving a thin beep as it moved away.

I walked to the nearest shop, where I stocked up on dried meat, some fruit and bread, and stuffed it all into my rucksack. But as I walked away from the till, the cardboard case holding my wine ripped, and two of the three bottles of the wine that Martin had given me smashed on the floor. I found my way to the train station disheartened at having lost my gift, and because dropping the bottles felt like I'd started a run of bad luck.

I got off the train in a small mountain town called Bardonecchia, just over the border in Italy, with wood and stone buildings nestled into pine woodlands. The sun was setting, so I picked a spot in the surrounding woods that I could see from the train station and walked towards it up a thin concrete road. As I moved away from the town centre, the houses thinned out. When I felt that I was far enough away, I veered off the concrete path and walked into the woods, trying to keep in a straight line so I could find my way back to the road in the morning. I found a small clearing and put my tent up. Then I undressed and bedded down into my sleeping bag to eat a quick meal of bread and fruit. As it was by that point dark, I tried to sleep, but couldn't manage it. At the vineyard I had been working twelve hours a day and finished each evening exhausted. Without that exertion, I didn't feel tired.

I had been lying awake for perhaps an hour when I heard something in the woods. I'd been listening to some gentle rustling, which I thought was probably just a bird, but after a while the rustling built into what sounded like something crashing through undergrowth. Then silence followed, and then the crashing started up again. I thought back to the town I'd passed through to get to this spot. It had felt like some of the locals had been watching me as I'd passed the local bar, and they must have seen where I was headed. The road hadn't forked or changed once since I left the town, and I reasoned that if they had wanted to find me, all they'd have to do was follow that one path. I had probably left pretty obvious tracks where I had entered the woods. The sound I was hearing could have been someone close by moving around in the dark.

Before I'd left for my trip, a friend had given me a kind of Swiss Army knife that made up a dining set. It unfolded into a knife and fork and detached into two so you could use them separately. The fork was probably sharper than the knife. I unfolded it so that both knife and fork were pulled out but still attached to one another. I lay holding my weapon to my chest, staring at the roof of the tent. The silent patches between the rustling and crashing seemed to shorten, and I was sure that whatever it was, was getting closer. Eventually, some component of my resolve gave way, and I whipped the tent flap back and jumped out, completely naked, with my knife-fork raised above me. I walked around the surrounding woodlands, but whatever was stalking me obviously did not have the courage to show itself. Out of ideas, I returned to my tent, muddying up the inside with the dirty soles of my feet.

My attacker was clearly playing the long game. Not long after settling back down, the rustling started up again, and after a while I couldn't lie there anymore and jumped out a second time, but with my torch. I held the knife-fork in my right hand, ready to strike, and the torch in my left. I slipped on my shoes and did a thorough search of the area, finding nothing. I returned to my tent and was pulling the tent flap back when I heard a crash behind me. I spun round like a madman slashing at the air unidirectionally: fork then knife, fork then knife; but I hit only thin air.

I went back to my tent door and crouched down, surveying the area. When I couldn't see anything, I was forced to consider that it was just wind, or an animal that had no interest in me, or that I was going insane and should probably just have gone to sleep. But by then I'd lost my nerve, and the inside of my tent was completely turned over. There were footprints made by my muddy feet on my sleeping bag. After some deliberating, I got dressed, packed up my tent and walked back to Bardonecchia to look for a hotel.

11

Jungle Junction

Sudan to Kenya—Four

George and I had to wait at the petrol station in Nairobi for around an hour before the tow truck turned up. The kids who had helped push us had gone, but one of the mechanics who worked at the garage wouldn't leave us alone. George refused to engage with him, so he focussed on me. He kept on talking about how he was the boss. "I'm the daddy, here. The boss. Not just here but this whole street." He kept saying it. I gave him a cigarette and he went away for a while before coming back. He was a big man and he got into your personal space to speak to you. I couldn't understand what he wanted.

The tow truck arrived. It was an ancient black Land Rover with a winch on the bed. The tow truck driver shook everyone's hands, including the mechanic's, and we helped him attach George's truck. It was agreed that George would steer our Hilux, as he was the more experienced driver, and I would travel in the Land Rover. As we got into the cab, the mechanic started speaking faster and begged for money. I slipped a note through the window quickly, so that George wouldn't see.

The Land Rover was more like a tank inside. The gear stick had no cover, and you could see the mechanics of it moving as the driver changed gears. The engine made noises like a tugboat as it pulled us uphill. We made our way out of the city centre into suburbia, where plump hedgerows surrounded large, ornate houses. In the cooling twilight you could have been fooled into thinking you were in Southern England.

It was dark by the time we reached the campsite, called Jungle Junction, that also had a garage where travellers got their vehicles serviced before heading further south. I'd read online that a few years earlier the campground had been targeted by armed criminals who had held both the owner and several of the guests tied up as hostages for an entire night as they robbed the place. Since then, security had been increased, and to get into the campsite you had to pass through a huge steel gate that opened remotely after giving your identity through the intercom system.

The truck driver got out and spoke through the intercom, and the steel gates opened so we could enter. He pulled us into the car park, unhooked our truck, took his fee and left after shaking both our hands. The owner of the camp came out to greet us and showed us around, pointing out a beer fridge, which was paid for using an honesty box, and a communal seating area where a handful of guests sat. Two of them were a Canadian couple George and I had met in both Sudan and Ethiopia, so when our tour was finished, we bought a beer from the fridge and went to sit with them. We told them about our journey into the city, about how the car had broken down and how the local kids had pushed us, and about the night before that we had spent with the soldiers at their barracks. The couple said that on the outskirts of Nairobi they'd been put up by some Kenyan soldiers too.

We hadn't been able to use phones or the Internet for a few days, so I went and dug my laptop out from the truck and got it going. When I accessed my email account, I had one from my mum. It began:

Jay, this is the hardest email I've ever had to write. Your father has been diagnosed with lung cancer.

The next day I left George for the airport to fly home. I had hired a taxi through the campsite, and after I loaded my stuff into the boot, we hugged each other.

"Look after yourself, please mate," I said.

"Well, I'll fucking have to now, won't I?" said George.

And I noticed his eyes were wet, and I was surprised and felt fresh regret for leaving him, so we hugged again, and then I climbed into the taxi and started towards the airport.

My driver was called Declan. When I told him I was cutting my trip short to return home because my dad had lung cancer, he was sympathetic. He told me that his father had died when he was sixteen.

"And what about your mother?" I asked.

"She had died two years before that."

"So, were you alone?" I asked him.

"No, I had my sisters."

"Were they older than you?"

"No, they were two and five years junior to me."

"So did you have to look after them?"

"Yes, I had to provide for them."

"That must have been very difficult for you," I said.

"Yes," he said, "but in life you have to be strong."

156

12

This is The Place

Kayaking With My Brother

The day before setting off, I had finished my second year of university. I'd been spending five days a week on placement in Critical Care and writing up assignments in the evening, often into the night. If you'd asked me, I wouldn't have been able to tell you how many hours I'd sat at my desk. I was desperate to be somewhere else for a while. My brother needed a break too, and together we started planning a kayak trip. If we wanted to leave the UK, it was going to mean driving a long way. My car was in bad shape, a death trap really, but if it was to be my only escape the risk was worth it.

The idea of me travelling long distances in my knackered car worried Rishni. She tried to get me to take her car instead, which was much larger and more reliable, but that would have left her driving my old banger over the summer, so I refused. It had been a tough year for her too. She'd finished her first year as a teacher and had hated every minute of it, and at the end of the year decided to leave her job entirely. I didn't want to add to her problems by taking her transport away on top of all that. I felt like a cad leaving her alone that summer anyway, but we agreed to talk daily. When it was time for me to leave, she came with me to my car and stood on the curb, waving as I drove away.

From the first moment I bought my car, it made a high-pitched whine whenever the motor was running. The pitch got higher the faster I drove. I travelled the two hundred and thirty-eight miles from my home in Sheffield to East Wittering in Sussex with the whine at medium pitch, as my mechanic had told me not to take the car over fifty miles an hour. Apparently, fifty was a good maximum speed. To go any faster may have caused some vital component in the car's structure to disintegrate. If this happened, the car would "sort of go like that," the mechanic had said while moving his hands in opposite directions—one up, one down—to describe, I suppose, my car flipping over spontaneously.

I was going to pick up a second-hand kayak that my brother, Jack, was buying online. Once I'd got it, I was going to head to Devon, where I'd pick up my father's old kayak. Then I'd drive with both the boats to catch a ferry to Ireland. Jack was still working for the next few days and was going to fly out to Ireland to meet me there. All in all, I had around seven hundred miles to drive in a car that couldn't travel over fifty miles an hour.

As I drove south, the day kept getting hotter. Whenever the car thermostat reached thirty degrees Celsius the engine started overheating. I got stuck in traffic on the M40 and had to have my heater on full blast to keep the engine cool. Somehow, I'd forgotten to bring water, and I looked through my window at the vehicles stuck in traffic next to me, with air conditioning and well-hydrated drivers, and considered leaning out the window to ask if they had a spare drink for me. I could feel a layer of congealed sweat on my skin, and my hair was wilted and damp. Just after I'd passed through Chichester there was a diversion due to some kind of accident. A group of overweight, middle-aged women in high-visibility jackets were dotted around the town helping to direct the traffic.

By five o'clock I'd finally made it to Pete's house. Pete was the man selling Jack his kayak. We'd been in contact over the last few days to organise the collection.

"I'll tell you what, you've done fucking well," Pete said in a jaunty Cockney accent as he came around the corner of his house to greet me. He was older and shorter than I had thought he would be. He could have been seventy, with crow's feet and short, grey hair, and he walked with his shoulders pulled back, his arms swinging and bowed. "Was it a fucking nightmare getting in?" he asked as we shook hands.

"It wasn't too bad, in comparison to the motorway," I said. "There was a diversion, but there were some volunteers guiding us into the town."

"We've had a woman drown just a mile down the road, and another lad was just finishing work and got hit by a tractor," he said. "Within five minutes of each other."

Pete took me into his house, and I said hello to his family, who were sitting at the table eating a roast dinner. We walked through the house and out into the garden, where he brought me a cup of tea and a jar of biscuits, which I ate ten of, one straight after the other. As I ate, Pete took the kayak out of the shed and told me about the trouble he'd had trying to sell it.

"It's as good as fucking new, I've only taken it out twice," he said. "One chump, a student—foreign student—rang me up and wanted to give me three hundred quid for it. I told him no way, it's seven hundred quid new, I won't take less than five fifty. And then a few days later he called me up and told me he had three hundred quid and a stereo that he wanted to give me for it. I told him that if he wants it, then he'd have to pay me the fucking money. Simple as that."

The weather was cooling as I checked the kayak over, and with Pete's help put it on top of my car. It was over a metre longer than my Yaris and hung over the back. I had to measure up with a tape measure to make sure I wasn't liable to get pulled over by the police if they saw me.

Pete talked like a scattergun while we worked, describing how the boat had been designed to be attached to a car, but we struggled getting the kayak tied down at the front and back of the Yaris. He showed me how he used to attach it to his own car, but he was struggling to remember the exact knot. As I was fiddling with the ropes, I heard Pete have a breakthrough.

"Fucking hell, I'm getting good at this," he shouted from behind the car. As we lashed the kayak down, Pete's neighbour arrived.

"Did you struggle getting in?" he asked her. "We had a woman drown just up the coast a bit, and then a local lad got killed by a tractor on his way home. That was five minutes after the woman."

Between us we got the boat tied down. Pete's tour of the kayak was punctuated by a separate tour of the area. He pointed out where he took his kayaks and where he walked his dogs. Pete had grown up in South London but had moved to East Wittering two years prior.

"I had just had enough," he said. "London's changed. I used to know everyone, all my neighbours. Not anymore. Dare I say it?" Then he shook his head and said, "Dare I say it?" again, but apparently, he didn't. "I just couldn't be fucked with it. The rat race."

The coastline looked almost like Southern France to me, with its tall, dry grass and sand dunes bordering the beach. I shook Pete's hand goodbye and got in the car and back onto the road.

Two days later, I left Devon with two kayaks on the roof of my Yaris and made my way to Liverpool. I'd booked a ferry from Liverpool to Ireland that left the same night, so I had to make the journey in good time. It was still hot, and I had the same problem with the overheating engine as I drove, so I travelled slowly. It was dark by the time I got to the docks, but I was the first car there. To kill time, I sat in the car and called my mum and then my brother, and then watched the other cars fill the spaces around me. I also made a handmade GB sign with a biro and some writing paper I had in the boot, as I had read online that I legally needed a sign that identified the car as British in order to drive it in Ireland. I stuck the sign to my rear window.

After a while, we were beckoned through a gate where we showed our tickets and passports before being told to wait in another car park. I sat there for a few minutes before two police officers arrived and started talking to the drivers. I heard them asking for ID. Eventually, the male police officer made his way to my window.

"Can I see some ID feller?" he said. I showed him my passport, which he took but held without opening. He nodded to the kayaks and said, "So, it's a silly question, but I'm guessing you're going for a bit of a paddle?" He was a small man with a brown moustache. His voice was thin.

"Yep."

"I used to paddle a lot. I competed too. Do you compete?"

"I haven't, no."

"I used to take part in the slalom."

"Why did you stop?"

"The wife didn't like the amount of space it took up in the garage." His eyes lingered on the boats before he started flicking through my passport. He seemed to struggle to find my photo page. His brow furrowed.

"What were you doing in East Africa?"

"Just travelling. A friend and I went on a road trip across the northeast of Africa."

"It's just that you've got this Russian visa too," he said. At this point his colleague, a female police officer, stuck her head in through the window, scowling in hatred and confusion. It was a look that said I didn't matter at all.

"What do you do for work?" the male police officer asked me.

"I'm a student nurse at the moment," I said. "I don't travel for work, I just like travelling. I've been to Norway and France twice since East Africa. If they gave you a stamp whenever you travel in Europe, my passport would be full."

He gave back my passport, seemingly satisfied, and wished me good luck kayaking. His colleague walked away without saying a word.

As soon as the ferry docked I got out of Dublin. I drove the three hours northwest towards Dowra, a small, remote village not far from Shannon Pot, which is the source of the River Shannon. I wanted to get an idea of what the river looked like before Jack arrived in two days' time. That way, I could start planning the journey onwards.

I followed the sat nav on my phone, travelling mostly along

the N3, which is a thin road that passes through a hundred small, stretched-out towns. I stopped once to get some food but left empty-handed because everything in the shop was so expensive. I pressed on to a town called Virginia, where I was directed to a Lidl and bought some bread, fruit, eggs, butter and Irish black pudding, which I cooked and ate at a lay-by along the way. I was hoping to see some hitchhikers, thinking I could repay some of the help that was given to me and Imre a few summers earlier, but I didn't see anyone, even though I'd heard that Ireland was a good place for hitchhiking.

Dowra was a true agricultural village; the antithesis of the modern high street. The pavements and roads were grey, wet and muddy, and many of the houses looked empty. The buildings were brightly coloured, and I could make out some faded advertisements for bakeries and pubs painted on bright purple and bright blue walls. But a lot of the businesses were closed down with their windows boarded up. In the centre of the village there was a convenience store, a pub that was also a petrol station and a building called Keegan's, which advertised itself as an auctioneer, valuer, estate agent, funeral director and undertaker. I looped around the town and parked my car in what looked like a car park and walked to the pub. When I got to the door I stopped and listened a moment. It was so quiet inside that a part of me didn't want to go in.

Inside, the place was empty except for the barman, who stood behind the bar watching a TV in the corner. He was probably no older than nineteen. I ordered a Coke and sat down. The barman told me his name was Justin, and we started an awkward and halting conversation. His thick accent made it hard for me to understand some of what he was saying. He asked me what brought me to Dowra, the whole time looking as if he was about to break into laughter.

"My brother and I are going to kayak down the River Shannon," I said. "I'm here first, to bring the boats over, and he flies in the day after tomorrow, to Knock Airport."

"Down the River Shannon?" he asked. "The whole way?" I told him that was the plan. "That's a long way that you've got to kayak. How long do you think it will take you?"

"Two weeks," I said.

"And where are you staying tonight?"

"I'll find somewhere to put my tent."

"Yes, I think you'll be fine. I don't think that anyone will bother you."

"I hope not. I've never been bothered yet," I said and touched the wooden table in front of me. "Do you do that in Ireland too? Touch wood?"

"Yes, we do," Justin said. "To keep luck on your side?"

"Yeah."

"And does it work out for you?"

"I think it has so far. I feel as if I have pretty good luck."

"You shouldn't say that when you're getting ready to set off. This whole trip might go wrong for you now."

We kept talking as I drank my Coke. Every now and then Justin would see a car pull up to the petrol pump and run out to take the money, which went into the same till as the beer money. He told me he was a student at NUI Galway, where he was studying to become a teacher, but that he had grown up in Dowra and came home during the summer holidays to work in the pub. Dowra was a small place, where only thirty or forty children attended the local school. The town stayed quiet until the weekend, when there was a cattle market, and then the pub did good trade. After finishing my drink, I said goodbye to Justin and left, telling him I'd try and come back once I'd found a place to camp.

First, I went to the river to find a spot Jack and I would be able to launch our kayaks from, but when I got to the bridge and looked over the side into the water, I saw that it was six inches deep at best: I could make out the speckled patterns on the stones under the flow of the water. I went back to my car, picked up my camping gear and jumped over the closest hedge into a field to see if I could find somewhere to put my tent.

It had been raining while I was in the pub, and as I walked around the outskirts of Dowra with my camping stuff, I passed through fields and got wet feet from the grass. I couldn't find anywhere flat. I kept hopping over fences and searching through fields, but the ground was either all on a slant or covered in cow shit and thistle. Eventually, I found a spot that was flat enough and settled for it, despite being exposed on the top of a hill, pitching my tent in hope that the wind wouldn't pick up. As I burrowed into my sleeping bag, I felt the mixture of loneliness and depression that I always get on the first night camping alone in bad weather.

The next morning the weather had improved. I packed my tent up and went back to the pub so I could charge my phone. When I got through the door, I saw two old boys drinking Guinness at the bar; they glanced awkwardly at me as I walked in. Unlike the day before, the pub was nearly full, with people sitting down eating and a barmaid taking orders for drinks; Justin went about taking orders for food with a waiter's notebook. I ordered a coffee from the young woman and turned to the men drinking Guinness.

"Hello," I said.

"Hello..." said the younger one. The older guy just nodded. They were both flushed red from the beer and looked uncomfortable speaking to me. "...and welcome to Dowra," the young man finished, and they both offered me their hands to shake. We got talking, only I couldn't understand a lot of what they were saying. They had thick accents that were made harder to understand by drinking. At one point, the younger of the two asked what I was doing in Ireland. When I told him, he said—in the musical tone of voice you get when you repeat something you were taught in school fifty years ago, "The River Shannon starts at Shannon Pot, as just a trickle, and it goes on to Limerick, lasting for two hundred miles, which makes it the longest river in the British Isles."

The two men got talking to Justin, and I could understand enough to know that they were talking about a particularly large cow one of them had. I drank my coffee and, deciding to go, made a round of handshaking to say goodbye. I waited while Justin finished serving a table so I could shake his hand too.

I headed for a local campsite I'd found on Google Maps. It was a country road, but it was new and incredibly smooth; after a while, the tarmac turned to gravel, which crunched as I rolled up the track to the campsite. When I got to the reception there was a man outside eating what looked like ribs. He chewed as he walked over to my car, and I wound down the window. He asked me if I was OK.

"I was actually looking for somewhere I could put my tent," I said. "I know that you're advertised as a glamping site, but I wondered if you sometimes took tents as well?"

"We have done," he said, "but I wouldn't have anywhere for you to put it; we're fully booked at the moment. I don't know where your car would go either."

"That's fine. I thought I'd ask. Do you know anywhere locally that I could camp?" He sucked some meat from his teeth as he thought.

"There's a local spot on the lake, a cove with a little beach, you could camp there fine. We do sometimes. Where is it that you're planning on going?" He had a slight Yorkshire accent.

"I'm waiting for my brother to arrive and then we're going to kayak the Shannon down to Limerick," I said. He crouched down and looked through the window of my little car and nodded at me, smiling a little. I introduced myself and we shook hands. He said he was called Russ. He looked at my boats, and I got out to look with him. Russ told me that he'd helped a pair of Canadians do the same trip a few years before. They'd launched from the jetty at the bottom of his garden. He wanted to know how I planned on getting back to my car once I'd gotten to Limerick.

"I'm not sure yet," I said. "There's a kayak club in Limerick, and I was hoping that we'd be able to keep our boats with them while I make my way back up. I've noticed that there aren't many buses up this way though. I've thought about hitchhiking."

"Yeah, you might be able to," he said. "I did it when I first came over years ago, only I was with an attractive blonde, which helps."

"Oh yeah? Well, I think I'm out of luck there."

"You never know; she's inside the house, she might come with you." Russ then turned to the grass and pointed. "Alright, you can put your tent over there, on the grass. The kids play football there, but I don't think anyone will be playing football tonight. You can use the shower. Do you eat pizza?"

"Yes."

"We're having pizzas tonight," he said. "If you'd like one, I can put some extra dough in for you. And when you go to get your brother, you may as well keep the boats here to save some fuel. Where were you planning on leaving your car while you're kayaking?"

I told him I didn't know. "I'll find some space for it here on the drive," he said. "Just leave your keys with me so I can move it if I need to."

In the communal area of the campsite, Russ's wife Lucy helped me and the other guests roll out dough for the pizzas. We ate them next to a fire Russ had built in a big iron dish he'd recycled from old sheet metal. When we had finished, I stayed up talking about the Mayweather-McGregor fight with a young couple, Fionn and Tanya, who were staying in one of the yurts. Tanya worked for a company that focussed on entire body-mind wellness through a weight-lifting regimen and the removal of carbohydrates from the diet. Short and broad-jawed, Fionn told me that while working in the United States, he had once knocked his boss unconscious for making a bigoted remark about the Irish. I absolutely believed him. Nearby was an Irish family who were getting very drunk. Tanya couldn't stand them. I had bought Russ and Lucy a bottle of wine as a thank-you, and halfway through the night I saw one of the men, leaning back very drunk in his chair, struggling to open it.

Towards the end of the night, Fionn went and got a Cuban cigar that I didn't really want but we shared anyway. Fionn could pick out a thousand flavours in it that I couldn't. At one point, he said, "I think that you guys leaving the EU is a good thing for us in Ireland. It means that we've got another choice. I've never been completely convinced by the European Union."

And then Tanya walked back to her yurt, falling in the dark and hitting her face on the floor. When Fionn went to comfort her, I said goodnight and went to my tent.

I met Jack at the airport, which sat on top of a hill with a long, winding road running up to it. It was a small building, but the way it was placed made it look grand. Driving up the road felt like approaching a monastery. I could see Jack as I walked over to him—six foot three with his rucksack on one shoulder and mass of black hair. He was scanning the cars for one that looked like mine. I shouted to him, and he ran over to me; then we both ran back to where my car was parked to avoid paying the two euros charged for parking longer than fifteen minutes. As we ran, I shouted, "There's two euros on the line, Jack! Two euros!" The run was jubilant; it was sunny, and I had the feeling of true adventure—where you're slightly dirty, or hungry, and you know that to make whatever you're doing work, you're going to have to forget about things like washing or eating properly for a while.

I told Jack about Russ as we drove an hour and a half across remote woodland and farmland to Russ's campsite. Jack couldn't believe that in one day I'd met someone who could solve all of the logistical problems we'd been fretting about for months, and that he didn't want any money. All just because he was a nice guy and liked what we were doing. As we drove and talked, the road became dicey. In that part of Ireland, the roads were built to fit two cars, one travelling in either direction, but the foliage on either side spilled onto the road, making it hard to see what was coming from further up. There was no room to overtake, but people did anyway. At one point we were nearly killed by a car overtaking a tractor on a corner. It sped towards us head on, passing the tractor, then swerved back onto the other side of the road, missing us by a metre.

When we got to Russ's, we went to the house so I could introduce Jack to Russ and his family, and then we loaded the kayaks onto the roof of the Yaris. It was getting late by this point, so we decided to camp on the edge of Lough Allen and get moving early in the morning. Before we left, Russ told me that if I dropped the car off at his place the next morning, he'd be able to drop me back down before we set off.

It took a while to find the cove. There were a few paths leading to smaller beaches, but none of them could have accommodated the car. Eventually, we found the entrance and travelled down a narrow path that opened onto a concrete square. Behind the square was a beach that ran along the side of the lough, which was blue and placid but big enough that it could have been opening out into the sea. Around the lough, green hills hugged the water.

"Is this the place?" said Jack, and then when the concrete square opened up seamlessly onto the beach itself, just like Russ had described it, he said, "Yeah, this is the place."

At the cove we set up the tents and I pulled out all our gear. A lot of it was mine, but Jack brought dry bags and chargers for our phones that I wanted to get used to, so I gave it all a test run.

"I've been thinking," I said. "I've done a lot of trips like these now. I've got some experience in organising them. Do you think I could maybe start a business as a consultant for people who want to organise their own mini adventures?"

Jack said why not. I said it would make me an adventure consultant. I liked the title.

The gear was largely what I had used on previous trips, only

Jack had a duplicate of each item, and everything was in kayak bags. To navigate, we planned to use the navigation apps on our phones, but as a backup I'd made a rudimentary guide from a collection of other maps I'd found online. Each of us had a compass that we wore around our necks, along with our phones, which we kept in waterproof bags on a cord. In our jacket pockets we each had a lighter and some cotton wool wrapped in waterproof plastic, and a space blanket in case we lost a boat and needed to stay warm. We got into our wetsuits and put on some cheap wetsuit shoes I had bought last minute before setting off from Devon. Jack's were baby blue and seemed way too long for him, protruding like flippers at the bottom of his long legs and thin ankles. With his floppy hair, he looked like a Dr. Seuss character. I couldn't look at him without laughing. I told him that if I ever did get a job as an adventure consultant, he could be my right-hand man. Jack flapped his feet around with his hands on his hips and eyes narrowed like a war vet. "I only come in for the big jobs," he said.

It was getting dark, but we tested the kayaks. Jack's was very fast, faster than mine. Mine was steady though. It had been Dad's fishing kayak, and the wide bottom meant I could move freely while seated without the kayak tipping. It felt good to be out on it. I told Jack that I wished we could have been able to tell Dad about the lough. He could have come over and fished there. He would have loved it. There was nowhere in England where you could have had a place like that all to yourself.

The next day I dropped the car off at Russ's and he drove me down to the cove and left us to it; I felt that he could sense we wanted it to be just us two when we launched the boats for the first time. We got our gear packed up and launched the kayaks, running into the water to push them. Our legs sank into the silt as we ran, but we got the kayaks out of the shallows and hopped into them no problem. We pulled on our spray skirts and started paddling.

The lough was surrounded by dramatic hills. The weather was good. Jack said, "Yeah. Yeah, this is the way to travel," and I agreed with him. Then we pushed on. To Drumshanbo, and then to Killaloe, and then on to the rest of the two hundred miles towards Limerick. We had a good feeling about Limerick.

Printed in Poland
by Amazon Fulfillment
Poland Sp. z o.o., Wrocław